THE INTERNATIONAL BOOK OF

# LOFTS

# THE INTERNATIONAL BOOK OF
# LOFTS

## SUZANNE SLESIN
## STAFFORD CLIFF
## DANIEL ROZENSZTROCH

WITH PHOTOGRAPHS BY GILLES DE CHABANEIX
AND ILLUSTRATIONS BY ROBIN MASON

*Clarkson N. Potter, Inc./Publishers*
NEW YORK

# DEDICATION
## TO: JOACHIM BENO STEINBERG, ANDREW CLIFF, AND LAZARE ROZENSZTROCH

# ACKNOWLEDGMENTS

About five years ago, Jane West, the late publisher of Clarkson N. Potter, suggested that it would be a good idea to put together a book on the development of lofts. Although it has taken us longer to go ahead with the project than we had expected, we are grateful to Jane for her prescient suggestion and hope that we have produced a book she would have been pleased with.

We would like to thank all the people whose homes appear in the book as well as the many editors and writers who have published or written about some of the lofts we have chosen to include. Particular thanks are due to Nancy Newhouse, Dona Guimaraes and Carrie Donovan at the *New York Times* for their continual support and enthusiasm for the lofts movement. And also to Marilyn Bethany of *New York Magazine*, Christa Von Hantelmann of *Architektur und Wohnen*, and Daniel Lattes, Gabrielle Pascal, and Jean Girbas of *La Maison de Marie Claire*.

In addition, we are grateful to the assistance and enthusiastic help of John Scott, Don Goodwin, Nigel Holmes, Liese Howard and Andrew Pettit. To Judith Harte and Anne Dobel for proof-reading, Ian Hammond for the production artwork, and Robin Mason who did the drawings on the introduction pages.

Many thanks also to the photographers, especially to Gilles de Chabaneix, Robert Levin, Antoine Bootz, Tim Street-Porter, Ken Kirkwood, and Marco de Valdivia, whose work is included in the book, and to our research associates Inda Schaenen and Terri Cafaro.

We are, as always, indebted to our agent Lucy Kroll; and to the continued support and help of our editor Nancy Novogrod, as well as our publisher Carol Southern and Michael Fragnito, Gael Towey, Harvey-Jane Kowal, Teresa Nicholas and Jonathan Fox at Clarkson N. Potter.

Suzanne Slesin, New York
Stafford Cliff, London
Daniel Rozensztroch, Paris.
February 1986

# COPYRIGHT

Published by Clarkson N. Potter, Inc., 201 East 50th Street, New York, New York 10022. Member of the Crown Publishing Group.

CLARKSON N. POTTER, POTTER, and colophon are trademarks of Clarkson N. Potter, Inc.

Manufactured in Japan

Library of Congress Cataloging-in-Publication Data
Slesin, Suzanne.
The international book of lofts

Includes index.
1. Lofts–Remodeling for other use. 2. Architecture, Domestic. I. Cliff, Stafford. II. Rozensztroch, Daniel. III. Title.
NA7882.S54  1986  728.3'14  86-46
ISBN 0-517-56016-X
10 9 8 7 6 5 4 3
First Edition

# CONTENTS

# INTRODUCTION

Loft living represents one of the major trends in urban redevelopment in the last 30 years. The conversion of warehouses and factories into middle-class residences has meant not only a change of direction in the migration to suburbia and a revival of city centers that have fallen into decay, but also, maybe more important, the growth of a new consciousness.

In recycling commercial spaces into viable residences, loft dwellers express a respect for the urban past. This attitude has been in contrast with the general practice of developers who until recently often preferred to tear down abandoned buildings and on their sites erect modern and more commercial structures. The lofts revolution has been part of a movement that fostered the recognition of a city's architectural heritage and the value in preserving it.

New York's cast-iron buildings, many of which date back to the mid-19th century and are the work of James Bogardus; Paris's ornate glass-ceilinged "galeries"–the graceful grandparents of America's modern shopping malls; and London's dramatic stone and brick waterfront buildings are among the architectural types that have been rediscovered and reappreciated, and are being recycled into residential lofts.

The speed with which an area such as SoHo in New York has been gentrified tends to hide the early loft dwellers' long struggles. It has not been an easy route. Planning and zoning regulations have both protected and hindered progressive thinking. Many people lived and worked in sparse and uncomfortable lofts through years of illegality and harassment. It was not an uncommon experience for an artist who was living illegally as far as zoning regulations were concerned but with the consent of his landlord to find himself evicted after he had invested time, energy, and money in the renovation of his loft.

Early loft dwellers resorted to elaborate subterfuges in order to hide the fact that their loft spaces were being lived in–not simply used as studios. Beds were installed on pulleys that allowed them to be raised to the ceiling and hidden if a buildings or fire inspector came unexpectedly to call; groceries were not brought home in supermarket shopping bags; and residential garbage was frequently carried out of the neighborhood or hidden under artwork-related debris.

"Until the 1970s, living in a loft was considered neither chic nor comfortable . . . . Making a home in a factory district clearly contradicted the dominant middle-class ideas of 'home' and 'factory', as well as the separate environments of family and work on which these ideas were based," wrote Sharon Zukin in *Loft Living: Culture and Capital in Urban Change* (Baltimore, Md., The Johns Hopkins University Press, 1982).

More than any other element of lofts, it was probably their sheer physical space that ultimately overcame this resistance and gave birth to a new language of living in which homes were not described as a series of rooms, but rather as a number of square feet.

In the early 1970s, the demand for loft living spread beyond the downtown neighborhoods to the more traditionally minded members of the middle class who wanted space and were attracted to the new way of life that the location and expansiveness of lofts promised. Loft newsletters, loft cooperative boards, loft legalization, and the support of lawyers and business men, city planners and architects–some of them recent loft residents–made the public and city officials aware of the potential and power of the new movement. Municipal authorities finally recognized the viability of loft living and forced changes in zoning laws that allowed for the occupancy of the former factories and warehouses.

The downtown loft scene evolved from its bohemian and remote early status to include boutique- and restaurant-lined streets and many mixed neighborhoods where traditional shops and new businesses can for a short while still exist side by side. In the process, the formal and preordained living patterns that have seemed to constrain people since the last century have been brought into question. Changing attitudes toward domestic life are reflected in these living spaces, which can easily accommodate home offices or work spaces and can remain open or be divided depending on the needs of the residents.

Lofts continue to offer an exciting alternative to urban apartments and a way for individuals to express their personal views through the places in which they live. The lively spirit that propelled the lofts movement has reached beyond commercial neighborhoods and can easily be seen in the planning and construction of new houses and apartments and the renovation of existing ones. The influence is apparent in the layouts and floor plans that are being devised, with fluid spaces and rooms that tend to be more open to one another than in the past.

No longer experimental or even trendy, loft living is a fully established and accepted lifestyle that is bound to have an important and enduring effect on residential design.

# THE HISTORY OF LOFTS

Some of the spaces considered the ancestors of lofts today are artists' ateliers – custom-built studios with large-paned north-facing windows, which flourished in Paris as early as the mid-19th century and in New York at the turn of the century. The execution of overscale academic and military paintings required expansive high-ceilinged studios, and traditionally, painters were located on the upper floors of the buildings, while sculptors, whose materials and finished pieces were heavier and more unwieldy, were usually found on the lower or ground floors.

But what we more readily think of as lofts today are spaces originally occupied by such crafts and industries as woodworking, printing, belt and tie manufacturing, and cardboard box making in buildings that have been converted into residences. In Paris, these include factories, in culs-de-sac, and in courtyards behind apartment buildings.

Light industry often occupied entire floors set up with dozens of workers at long tables. In New York, the printing and publishing industries as well as clothing companies, which ultimately moved from Lower Manhattan to the center of the garment industry, or rag trade, on Seventh Avenue, were some of the most important of early loft tenants.

New York City's large architectural firms, numbering about 600 at the turn of the century, were also early tenants of loft buildings. The George B. Post firm, one of the most important in New York, was located on Union Square North, while many others were grouped along Broadway below 14th Street.

Loft buildings were concentrated, too, in areas of large cities that were near the docks and served for the storage and distribution of food stuffs. In Boston, New York's TriBeCa, and in both London's Covent Garden and Docklands areas, many loft buildings originally provided warehousing for cheese, spices, coffee, and tea.

The birth of residential loft living can clearly be ascribed to the SoHo area of Manhattan, where artists have occupied lofts since the late 1940s. It was the late 1950s, however, that saw the swift revitalization and the beginnings of gentrification of SoHo, the area between Houston and Canal Streets formerly known as Hell's Hundred Acres. The numerous fires and overcrowded conditions in this neighborhood had once been a prime target of the American Labor Movement.

Few loft dwellers today can ignore the irony of a single family living luxuriously in a 2,000-square-foot space that was in their parents' and grandparents' time the oppressive workplace of perhaps 200 people.

*LEFT: Cast-iron structures are mingled with tenement buildings in Lower Manhattan about 1910.*

**TOP:** Wooden shipping and storage barrels are stacked by New York's East River in an early 20th-century photograph of the Fulton Market. Originally a retail complex for the sale of meat and produce, the six blocks bounded by Fulton, Dover, Water, and South streets gradually became an important wholesale outlet for fish—and in recent years a tourist attraction and a residential neighborhood as well.

**ABOVE CENTER LEFT:** Pushcarts and horse-drawn wagons made their daily deliveries and pickups on Worth Street in New York's wholesale district near City Hall in about 1890. Situated between Broadway and Church streets,

Worth Street was lined with an impress- ive row of cast-iron warehouse build- ings, some built around 1869 by the architect Griffith Thomas. In the early 1960s, a large part of the block was des- troyed and replaced by a parking lot.

**ABOVE AND LEFT:** Awnings protected pedestrians from the sun and tramways were important means of public trans- portation along Lower Broadway at the turn of the century.

*LEFT AND BELOW LEFT:* Two French factory complexes at the turn of the century feature a series of low brick buildings with rounded window tops. Access was through a main gate and goods were transported on tramlike tracks. At left is a printing plant, the Imprimerie Crête-La Cour at Corbeil-Essones; the Emaillerie Parisienne, an enamel factory at Boulogne-Billancourt, near Paris, with workers posed near the main gate, is below left.

*RIGHT:* Huge metal strut walkways connected some of the warehouse buildings along London's Wapping High Street at the beginning of the century.

*BELOW RIGHT:* Built in 1884, by the Arbuckle Brothers, for the storage of green coffee beans, and shown in a 1936 photograph by Berenice Abbott, the warehouse was nestled under the Brooklyn Bridge. Now, the round-topped and shuttered openings have been filled in with glass and the structure, like many others in the neighborhood, has been converted into a loft dwelling.

*ABOVE:* A horse-drawn carriage stands in front of the A. T. Stewart store, which opened in 1859 on Broadway between Ninth and Tenth streets in New York City. The department store was considered to be one of the largest cast-iron structures ever built. On the exterior, glass windows were framed by a series of Corinthian columns. The interior was punctuated by cast-iron columns and wrought-iron beams, and the floors were laid out in circles around a rotunda topped by a glass skylight. A fire destroyed the wooden floors before the building was torn down in 1956.

*RIGHT:* An engraving depicts the A. T. Stewart sewing room in 1875. Although the store specialized in selling fabric for women to make clothing at home, it also sold garments hand-sewn by several hundred employees. The women worked at long tables in a large open space with cast-iron columns.

**ABOVE:** *In the huge loft of the Club Clothes factory in Buffalo, New York, garment workers are shown on the cutting room floor in the 1920s, before mechanization changed the industry.*

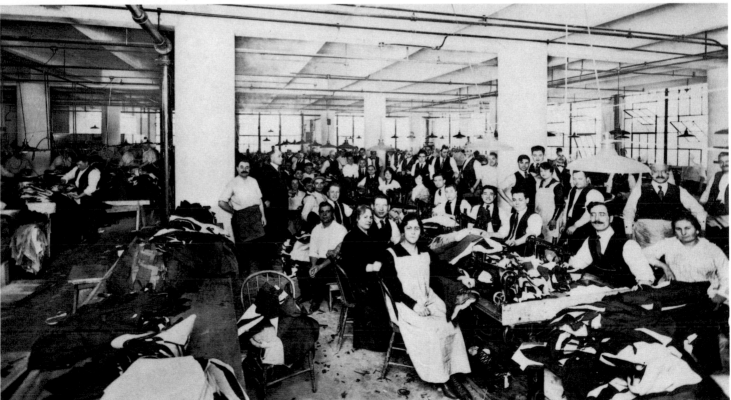

**TOP:** Men and women work side by side at tables at an unidentified dressmaking factory in the early 20th century.

**ABOVE:** Dozens of people labored together at long tables in the open loft spaces that characterized the Garment District of New York City in 1905.

**ABOVE:** *Large-pane metal-frame windows allow daylight into a work space where typesetters operate monotype machines which cast and set type in single characters, in about 1940.*

**ABOVE LEFT:** *Long metal beams span a Parisian loft factory space in which wooden tables and stools have been grouped around the steel columns.*

**LEFT:** *Rows of sewing machines are neatly lined up against a double wall of windows in a factory space in Paris.*

**RIGHT:** *A window-lined Paris loft was one of the spaces where workers made suitcases for Louis Vuitton, the French luggage company that has been in existence for four generations.*

**LEFT:** *A New York loft with wide-set columns served as the drafting offices for the architectural firm of G. B. Post in about 1900. George B. Post, one of the most acclaimed architects of the era, died in 1913, but the firm, located on Union Square North, continued under the aegis of the architect's sons.*

*LEFT AND RIGHT: Butler's Wharf, an 11-acre site located between Tower Bridge and St. Saviour's Dock, in Bermondsey on the south bank of London's Thames River, includes warehouses that date from the turn of the century. A center for the tea trade, the area was also used for the storage of grain, pepper, spices, fruit, cocoa, and sugar. The warehouses ceased to be active in 1972, and the riverside site is currently being converted into a residential, retail, and office complex.*

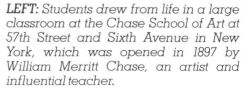

**LEFT:** Students drew from life in a large classroom at the Chase School of Art at 57th Street and Sixth Avenue in New York, which was opened in 1897 by William Merritt Chase, an artist and influential teacher.

**BELOW LEFT:** In 1925, students sketched in a drawing class at Paris's Ecole d'Arts Appliqués.

**BOTTOM LEFT:** McCall's magazine had an open space for commercial artists in 1912 when the publication was located at 236 West 37th Street.

**RIGHT:** A two-story 19th-century painter's atelier in Paris was filled with a collection of antique paraphernalia and fabrics used as models for large-scale academic paintings.

**ABOVE:** *An anonymous horse painter sketched in his atelier in France in 1908.*

**ABOVE LEFT:** *Between 1916 and 1922, when Claude Monet, the French Impressionist painter, was in his 70s, he worked on his Nymphéas series in a 3,000-square-foot studio at Giverny, near Paris. The large canvases, single panels of which extended to 19 feet, were placed on rolling bases in the enormous loftlike work space.*

**LEFT:** *Boarding school students painted at easels set up in front of a Mondrian-like window in a studio at the Pensionnat de la Providence at Bouzonville, France, at the beginning of the century.*

**RIGHT:** *In the late 1960s, The Factory, Pop artist Andy Warhol's famous East 47th Street Manhattan loft, was a center for art happenings. Pipes were left exposed and the brick walls were bare. Some of the stars of the movies that were made there included Ultra Violet, Viva, and Taylor Mead.*

# LOFT ATMOSPHERE

The atmosphere of loft neighborhoods contrasts sharply with that of more traditional residential areas. Instead of dry cleaners and grocery stores, one would be more likely to find corrugated box suppliers and machine repair and tool and dye shops. Streets are often lined with trucks and there is an absence of trees, parks, and playgrounds.

The loft buildings themselves—whether in London's Docklands, near Paris's Place de la Bastille, or in New York's SoHo or TriBeCa—are usually large structures with awesome, rugged exteriors that do not exude the familiarity, homeyness, and sense of stability of London's neat row houses, Paris's solid bourgeois apartment buildings, or New York's canopied apartment houses.

Whether on the waterfront, at the end of a cobblestoned alley, or in the middle of a still bustling warehouse area, loft buildings offer a different esthetic—unpolished, sometimes dingy and poorly maintained, and nearly always surprisingly different from the recently renovated and slickly furnished spaces inside.

Visitors are greeted by a puzzling array of doorbells; keys to freight elevators sent down in baskets on pulleys; and rows of mailboxes near bulletin boards crowded with neighborhood notices—some of the most telling details that indicate the newly residential aspect of the buildings. Steep wooden stairs leading to the upper floors look as if they could only be scaled by mountain climbers, but baby strollers, bicycles, and other signs of family life are parked on many landings.

*LEFT: In 1976, an architectural group toured cast-iron loft buildings in New York's landmarked SoHo district.*

23

*LEFT:* A residential loft in a 1910 building that used to house printing companies looks downtown over tenement rooftops in New York's Chelsea area.

*BELOW LEFT:* Situated at the end of a cul-de-sac, an industrial loft building in Paris's Bastille district offers a view of earlier structures.

*BOTTOM LEFT:* In Australia, near Sydney, a large factory and warehouse building has been converted into residential lofts.

*RIGHT:* Peeling paint, garbage bags, truck loading docks, and huge commercial signs are still present where industrial buildings are already beginning to be converted to residential use in New York's SoHo, TriBeCa, Chinatown, and West Side waterfront areas.

**LEFT:** *Old factories and warehouse buildings in London's Docklands, in the areas of Wapping, Limehouse, and Rotherhithe, are being converted into high-priced lofts and apartments.*

**RIGHT:** *Many of the buildings are of brick with the most famous of the structures, along a street called Shad Thames, connected to one another by a series of overhead bridges.*

*LEFT AND RIGHT:* A jumble of mailboxes inside the entrance door, steep wide stairs that lead vertiginously to the upper floors, office building lobbies, and security and telephone paraphernalia are all elements that identify newly residential lofts.

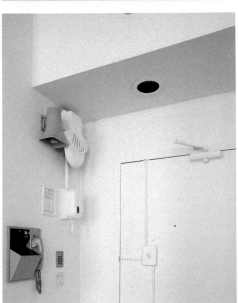

*RIGHT: Simple cast-iron columns dot the grand open space on the ground floor of Manhattan's Puck Building. Built by the J. Ottman lithographic company in 1885, and designed by the architect Albert Wagner, it eventually housed 30 lithographic presses and 400 employees and, in 1892, was the largest building in the world devoted to publishing. The cartoons that appeared in the witty Puck magazine, which began its publication in 1877, were printed there.*

*Puck ended its publication in 1918, and a number of printers and graphic firms occupied the building until recently. In 1982, the Puck Building was renovated into a commercial condominium for architects, designers, and filmmakers.*

# 3

# THE LOFT STATEMENT

There are few spaces that offer such a range of opportunity for making a design statement as empty lofts. Structural columns, gleaming white walls, exposed radiators, windows facing unexpected views, even the web of fire sprinkler pipes, are elements that gracefully integrate into the final interior. Unrenovated lofts have become the interior design laboratories of our time.

Often there have been no prior residential tenants in the space to leave their mark. And depending on spatial requirements or on desired effects, lofts are transformed into three-dimensional design statements.

There is not one loft look. Rather, the spaces lend themselves to styles that range from the minimal to the theatrical. Most are without architectural detailing to set the tone, so it is the spaces themselves – the long rows of windows, skylights, and unbroken expanses – that provide the design cues. And, more often than not, the loft statement is a personal and innovative response to the challenge of creating a new interior environment.

**LEFT:** *New York designer Robert Currie stripped the structural steel column in his West Village loft. The rugged surface contrasts with the smooth white walls.*

## Minimalist scheme

Once a furrier's showroom in New York's Chelsea district, the 1,850-square-foot loft was converted by designer Peter Andes into a residence and work space. Situated in a 1922 building, the space featured a series of contiguous windows and an 18-foot-wide by 86-foot-long columnless area that was limited only by structural pilasters and beams.

Although the loft was subdivided into enclosed areas for the kitchen, bathroom, and storage units, Andes wanted to keep the other spaces ambiguous and open to one another. Adding a series of zigzag or L-shaped Sheetrock partition walls, he created an intentionally asymmetrical layout. The metal doors and the sprinkler system were painted white to blend in with the glossy walls and ceiling, while the radiators, the galvanized-steel window frames, and the brushed-aluminum blinds were covered with aluminum paint for metallic accents. Gray carpeting covers the floor, and a leather-draped bed, a low table, and stacking chairs are practically the only furnishings.

*ABOVE: A bed covered in suede is in a corner of the loft. The exposed pipes are painted white to match the walls.*

*RIGHT: The expanse of gray industrial carpeting, the shiny, blank white walls, and the low furniture contribute to the minimal, almost Japanese scheme.*

# Art Deco inspired

Situated on lower Fifth Avenue in Manhattan and boasting 4,000 square feet, 42 windows, and a dramatic view of the Empire State Building, the double loft was the first place the owners saw when they were looking for a new home in Manhattan. It had once been a warehouse for an Oriental rug dealer.

The couple needed ample wall space to display big paintings – he is a prominent art dealer in New York – and a gracious expanse for entertaining. The public and private areas of the loft were to be separated.

"Because they were European and interested in Art Deco, I started thinking about transatlantic ships as a metaphor," explained Carmi Bee, the architect who was a partner in the firm of Brown & Bee when he designed the renovation of the loft.

To take full advantage of the 50-foot-long living room, the architect created a ceremonial entrance and built a series of levels that focuses attention on the view. "The trick was always to find a balance between the architecture and the art," Bee said.

Dale Long, a partner in Long-Seever, a New York interior design company, was consulted on the furnishings – a combination of modern and Art Deco pieces. The size of the space necessitated large-scale pieces. "Everything we had before was just too small," said one of the owners.

*ABOVE: A view of the Empire State Building is a feature of the loft.*

*ABOVE: A 1979 still life by Fernando Botero hangs at one end of the 50-foot-long living room.*

*LEFT: French cameo glass from the 1930s is displayed on shelves lining the window alcove.*

*BELOW LEFT: A bar unit separates the living and dining areas. The chairs, found in an upstate New York shop, were reupholstered in silk and edged in braid. The sconces once hung in the Biarritz salon of Jean Patou.*

*RIGHT: The mail chute dates from the building's commercial days. The 1911 bronze sculpture by the front door is Jacques Lipschitz's first piece.*

*LEFT:* Sliding mirrored panels act as a pass-through to the kitchen from the dining area, where leather-covered chairs surround a glass-and-chrome Dominique dining table that was made in France in the 1930s. The low-voltage hanging light fixture is a custom design, and the painting on the far wall is a 1979 oil on paper by Mark Rothko.

*BELOW LEFT:* The small kitchen features black laminate and white marble counters, a center work island, and a restaurant stove.

*RIGHT:* A drawing of a muscled arm by Dieter Hacker, a German artist, hangs in the playroom and exercise area.

*BELOW RIGHT:* In the master bedroom, the bed has been upholstered with an English chintz fabric. The armoire is a 19th-century French faux bamboo piece and the chaise is a late-19th-century antique. A collection of personal drawings lines the wall.

## Personal expression

Five years ago, before his recent success, Philippe Starck, one of France's most innovative and talented designers of furniture and interiors, lived in a Paris loft near the Grands Boulevards, with Brigitte Laurent and their daughter, Ara.

The interior of the loft, a former woodworking shop that had been used as a photographer's studio for the last few decades, had been totally gutted. The new space, filled with objects, represented a kind of contemporary bohemianism in which personal expression comes before sleek design.

*ABOVE AND RIGHT: A wood-burning stove has been installed in the sleeping area of the loft, where all the ductwork was left exposed.*

**ABOVE:** *Trinkets, spices, and cooking paraphernalia decorate the kitchen sinks, creating a kind of richly colored and textured Indian temple altar.*

*ABOVE:* A metal shade hangs on a
fishing-pole-like stick over the dining
room table. The champagne cooler
serves as a vase.

## Large and intimate

"Even though it's large in scale, I have an intimate feeling about the space," said Peter Carlsen, a journalist, of his New York loft, which was designed by Joseph Paul D'Urso. Carlsen added, "I see it as a transition between Joe's early minimal and later baroque phases."

Because it was intended for one person, the white-walled space was left fairly open. The 14-foot-high windows allowed for the inclusion of a mezzanine level and tall, thick columns created a striking rhythmic colonnade. A zigzag wall, a bookcase, a carpeted stair, and Carlsen's own collection of modern and vintage furniture pieces are the interior's decorative elements.

*ABOVE: Bookcases are nestled in a corner near the carpeted stair that leads to a small mezzanine sleeping area.*

*LEFT: A long zigzag wall delineates the space in a New York loft designed by Joseph Paul D'Urso. The Fledermaus chair is a Wiener Werkstätte design by Josef Hoffmann.*

**ABOVE:** *The plain white columns contribute to the classical simplicity of the interior. The small 1920s Art Deco table has been refinished in black lacquer and the chairs reupholstered in black leather. The red metal child's chair is a Japanese design.*

**ABOVE:** *The windows are shaded with flowing canvas curtains that are hung on metal rods. The chaise is by Le Corbusier, and the glass-and-steel table near the far window is one of D'Urso's early prototypes for Knoll International.*

## Multipurpose plan

To take maximum advantage of the 26-foot-wide and 100-foot-long loft situated on the top floor of a post-Civil War commercial building in Manhattan's Greenwich Village, Jack Lenor Larsen, the textile designer, opted for a large living space that would be suitable for entertaining crowds and could accommodate his many personal collections. Although there are no separate bedrooms, the loft offers multiple sleeping options – two daybeds that slide under storage units when not in use, and two raised platforms, one at each end of the loft.

"I was in Kyoto when I designed the loft and it was built by a Japanese contractor," Larsen explained, referring to both the esthetic of the space and its multipurpose plan. While handcrafted furniture is used throughout and some of the designer's objects are on display, many pieces, including his collection of contemporary British porcelains, are kept on shelves behind sliding partitions that line the walls. "That means that you don't have to look at everything all the time," Larsen explained. "And it also means that things don't get broken and are kept relatively dust free."

*ABOVE: Jack Lenor Larsen's loft is on the top floor of the building.*

*ABOVE: In the living room area, where the floor is covered with modern Italian ceramic tiles, a collection of porcelains is stored behind sliding partitions. The basket chairs are reproductions of a 1950 design by Nana Ditzel.*

**ABOVE:** *Handmade teakettles ranging from a tiny 15th-century Chinese design to contemporary pieces, are arranged on a low table by Dick Wickman, a Wisconsin craftsman and woodworker.*

**LEFT:** *A raised platform lines the skylit loft's rear windows. The folk art sculpture of two figures is by Edward Tolson.*

**ABOVE:** *Although it is made of Texas longhorn cattle horns, the chair is thought to be an 1880 Bavarian piece.*

**ABOVE:** *The cane-backed settee was designed by Ben Baldwin, an American designer, for Jack Lenor Larsen's firm.*

**ABOVE:** *A soaking pool has been installed in the platform by the windows. The white paper sculpture is by Bernadette Lamprecht, a Belgian artist.*

**ABOVE:** *The small balcony at the back of the loft has a southern exposure.*

## Mirror image

The basic idea behind the New York Garment District loft that belongs to R. Scott Bromley and Robin Jacobsen, the partners of Bromley/Jacobsen, an architectural and design firm, was to provide separate and private sleeping areas for the two occupants. "But we also wanted to take advantage of the light and view and keep the spaces as open as possible," said Mr. Jacobsen of the dramatic 2,100-square-foot loft that overlooks the entrance to the Lincoln Tunnel, the Javits Convention Center, and the Hudson River.

The loft features a spacious shared open kitchen/dining/living area that has been extended by a greenhouse enclosure. At either end of the living area are the bedrooms, mirror images of each other, and their bathrooms and dressing rooms. The use of slick and shiny materials and detailing—black glass, stainless steel, and granite, a helium-and-argon light fixture, anthracite-colored ceramic tile, and black leather furniture – contrasts with the rough exposed beams and ceiling.

A minicomputer-processor activates the motorized padded leather entrance, sliding doors that provide privacy for the two bedrooms, floor-activated light switches, and motorized shades for the north-facing skylight.

*ABOVE: The exterior of the converted factory features large windows.*

*ABOVE: A greenhouse enclosure dominates the main living space.*

*LEFT: In the east bedroom, a black column houses the digital controls for the lights and the sliding door panels. The glass-enclosed shower is situated directly behind the freestanding bed.*

*BELOW LEFT: Towels are stored on shelves near the plant-filled shower.*

*RIGHT: The west bedroom is adjacent to its own bathroom. The credenza holds the electronic controls.*

*BELOW RIGHT: A large window facing the view and an open shower are features of the tiled bathroom.*

*LEFT:* The helium-and-argon light fixture in the kitchen area mirrors the shape of the granite-covered counter.

*RIGHT:* The appliances have all been covered in black glass. The counter is used both as a cooking top and as a serving bar.

*BELOW RIGHT:* In one of the bathrooms, the sink is stainless steel.

## Theater set

About three years ago, David Rochline, a young musician, moved into what were once the offices of a small steel factory on the outskirts of Paris. "It was not my intention to do any kind of interior decoration," explained Rochline of the loft's striking, theatrical design scheme, which features trompe l'oeil painted floors and walls and an eccentric collection of furniture and props, some from theater sets Rochline created.

"There is no single modern element here," Rochline said. "And although it all looks rather special and different, it is the result of a logical and pragmatic point of view."

*ABOVE: The two-level loft is situated on the top floor of a small steel factory.*

*RIGHT: David Rochline, wearing a mask, poses among the furniture that dots the loft's open space.*

*LEFT:* The floor of the space has been painted in a trompe l'oeil marbleized checkered pattern.

*BELOW LEFT:* On the top floor, a wall-enclosed light well allows daylight to reach the floor below.

*RIGHT:* Candles and rumpled fabrics add to the theatrical atmosphere.

*BELOW RIGHT:* Gold damask draperies, velvet and brocade fabrics, and fanciful iron furniture are some of the decorative elements of the interior.

**ABOVE:** *Tambourines and fans are hung around the antique washbasin.*

**LEFT:** *The bedroom features a Venetian-style bed with a draped and painted headboard and an ornate French reproduction chest of drawers.*

# Made for the movies

It was primarily the extraordinary panorama – the view that encompassed the Brooklyn, Manhattan, and Williamsburg bridges, as well as Ellis Island, the twin towers of the World Trade Center, and the Statue of Liberty– that seduced Michael Cimino, the movie director. He used the Brooklyn industrial space as the residence for the star of his 1985 film *Year of the Dragon.*

The 3,200-square-foot loft was converted by Joseph Lembo and Laura Bohn of the Manhattan firm Lembo-Bohn Design Associates into a luxurious living place. The interior, with its uncurtained semicircular windows, softly carpeted floors, and understated furnishings that included a mix of antiques and modern pieces, represents the new potential for glamour in loft living. It replaces the intimate penthouse with a more youthful and dramatic image of the luxury city dwelling.

*ABOVE AND RIGHT: Panoramic views of the Manhattan and Brooklyn bridges provided a dramatic backdrop for the movie-set loft.*

**LEFT:** *Three television sets stood at the foot of the bed, which was situated a level above the living area.*

**BELOW LEFT:** *A pool-sized bathtub and shower were the focal point of the tiled bathroom. Three other small televisions provided bathtub viewing.*

**RIGHT:** *Low bookshelves acted as a divider between the living room and bedroom areas.*

**BELOW RIGHT AND BOTTOM RIGHT:** *The changes in the view by day and night gave the movie set an extra dimension of reality that would have been difficult to reproduce artificially.*

# THE ARTIST'S LOFT

Painters, sculptors, and performers – artists – were the pioneers of loft living. Driven both by economic need and by the physical requirements of their art, they were the first to explore, even homestead, neighborhoods and spaces that had been abandoned by commerce and industry. The desolate character of the buildings often suited the spirit of the work being produced.

Many of the existing features of even the most derelict industrial spaces made possible the works the artists wanted to create. Large and uninterrupted wall and floor surfaces could be used for stretching out canvases or assembling nearly monumental sculptures. Freight elevators, wide staircases, and indestructible floors allowed for the transport of heavy and unwieldy tools, materials, and finished works of art. And performance artists who had no access to more traditional theaters could develop their works and present them to reasonably large audiences.

Design solutions that are synonymous with lofts have frequently been invented by artists who use their carpentry skills and visual perceptions to renovate their studios. And it has become an accepted tradition for them to earn their living in the construction of lofts while waiting for their art to become salable.

The generous size and the unstructured nature of most loft spaces have allowed artists the freedom to set up personal creative environments that more traditional spaces would not. And another physical aspect of lofts that has been appreciated and put to good use is the unbroken surfaces they provide for artists to display many pieces at the same time – both to study their own works and as a way to exhibit their endeavors to dealers, clients, and critics.

*LEFT: A macaw perches on a pipe near the ceiling in artists Todd Miner and Judy Pfaff's New York SoHo loft. The yellow cubes are part of a work by Miner; the multimedia assemblage is a piece in progress by Pfaff. The floor, laid in a pattern with vintage vinyl tiles, was a collaborative effort.*

## Sculptor's studio

When Jane Rosen, a sculptor, moved to the 2,500-square-foot SoHo loft in which she has lived for the past 13 years, she decided to use the area with 14 nine-by-five-foot south- and east-facing windows as a living space and to place her studio in an interior section that would require artificial light. "I felt it was necessary to be able to control the light source," Rosen explained. The artist moves back and forth between the work and living areas.

Rosen kept the original space "pretty raw," only spending about $15,000 on plumbing, electrical work, and some construction. "I wanted the loft to be open, and a little funky and messy," she added. "It's like a big garage, filled with lots of objects I've collected that relate to work I've done or am thinking about. I don't like minimalism. I prefer to live with things that provide me with ideas."

*ABOVE: Jane Rosen stands near preparatory drawings and one of her marblelike wall reliefs.*

*ABOVE: A large table that is used for laying plaster and doing heavy work is situated in the center of the interior studio. The door leads to the sculptor's adjacent living area.*

*ABOVE:* The Texaco Flying A horse relief that has been hung above an overscale dresser is one of the objects the artist has collected because of the way it relates to her sculpture.

*ABOVE LEFT:* Old rattan lawn furniture was used in the light-filled loft.

*LEFT:* An antique stand-up radio and model boat were selected for their handcrafted features.

*BELOW LEFT:* The guest room includes a turquoise vinyl-covered beauty parlor chair from the 1930s that was found in a SoHo antique shop.

*RIGHT:* The open kitchen is furnished with a number of industrial objects that came from the neighborhood. An old wheel, suspended from the ceiling, has been converted into a pot rack; the often repainted table and chairs are used as color studies for the sculptor's pieces.

## Real-life inspiration

Janet Fish, the realist painter, has lived in the same loft building in New York's SoHo area for the past 11 years. Two years ago, she took over a lower floor and created a large studio space, but she continues to paint on both floors.

Her props are mostly glass bowls, plates, and tumblers of carnival glass that she has collected at lawn and garage sales and flea markets. The pieces are stored and stacked on a wall of bookshelves. "That's an easy way to see them all, so I can pick out the right color and shape for compositions," Fish said. The props are set up on tables or a windowsill. "I need to have a lot of daylight," Fish added. "Then I just keep looking at the things and painting them."

*ABOVE: Props are arranged against a window to simulate a beach scene.*

*LEFT: The large studio space is used for preparing and storing canvases.*

**ABOVE:** *The main living space is furnished with antique oak pieces.*

**LEFT:** *Multicolor crockery, a newspaper, and a nearly empty glass of orange juice have been assembled into a breakfast still life.*

**RIGHT:** *Bookshelves are used to store the artist's numerous props.*

**FAR RIGHT:** *A composition of glass decanters was set up on a windowsill.*

# Skylit work space

The sculptor who lived there in the 1950s had converted the 1,600-square-foot ground-floor apartment into a soaring artist's studio by removing the floor above and installing an enormous north-facing angled skylight. "I was fascinated – it looked like a huge, magical theater set," explained Alexander Vethers, an artist who moved to the unusual New York Chelsea loft from London. "Because of the light, it's a perfect working space," added Vethers, who stretches out his canvases in the huge open area that has 25-foot-high ceilings. Stairs at the rear of the space lead to a skylit bedroom and bathroom, while a dark-red-painted guest room and small kitchen that is adjacent to the garden on the main floor provide more enclosed intimate areas.

"I only used the shell," Vethers said. "I made no big alterations, but just painted it. This place already had a special aura and dignity. Modernizing it would have destroyed its character."

*ABOVE: A radiator that once belonged to the floor above now acts as an ad hoc sculpture over the fireplace. Large glass vases are lined up on the mantel. The ladders are for hanging canvases on the walls.*

*ABOVE LEFT: In the minimally furnished studio, a stack of pillows provides extra seating.*

*LEFT: An enormous angled skylight dominates the high-ceilinged studio space.*

**LEFT:** Near the kitchen, a pair of antique chairs, a sofa draped in white linen, and a folding table are used for dining.

**BELOW LEFT:** Copper pots and cooking utensils are displayed in the simple, all-white kitchen.

**BOTTOM LEFT:** The guest bedroom has been painted in red to provide a feeling of security and intimacy.

**RIGHT:** Simple bookshelves line one wall. The industrial fan and breezes from the garden keep the studio cool in the summer.

## Animal kingdom

Hunt Slonem, a painter, has lived and worked for the last 10 years in a loft overlooking a noisy corner of Manhattan's SoHo area. "That's one of the reasons I have all the animals," explained Slonem, who shares the space with what he described as "a lot of birds – a channelbill toucan named Augustus, a touraco, green-crested hornbills, Brazilian cardinals, troupials, laughing jay thrushes, green glossy starlings, Peking robins, red-breasted bluebills, many finches and quail."

Born in Maine, Slonem has spent time in Hawaii and Nicaragua, and has been collecting birds all his life. Now, many fly free in his loft and have become models for his paintings. There are also two skunks in the bedroom and seven turtles, and a lot of goldfish in the footed bathtub. "I observe them," Slonem said, "and they all influence my work."

The artist, who also does paintings of saints as well as large works depicting pre-Columbian gold objects, did very little renovation of the loft. "I built walls to hang paintings," he added, "and put in the bathtub that has now been overtaken by the fish. The whole place is a huge work space and I prefer to keep it pretty simple."

*ABOVE AND LEFT: Birds, used as models in the paintings, are often let out of their cages and allowed to fly free in the main studio area of the loft.*

**ABOVE:** *A tabletop painted in a religious theme serves as a bar.*

**TOP AND ABOVE:** *Large paintings are propped up against all the walls in the living room, which is furnished with white wicker pieces.*

**TOP:** *The artist's paintings of saints as well as his smaller portraits line the walls of the bedroom.*

**ABOVE:** *Gothic-style chairs surround the dining table, which is also used as a desk. The paintings on the wall are in a pre-Columbian gold theme.*

**ABOVE:** *In the bathroom, the tub is filled with goldfish.*

## On the horizontal

Having lived and worked in a typical high-ceilinged artist's studio for many years, Michel Gueranger, a young French painter and conceptual artist, wanted "to make a break with the myth of the artist and his studio," and he decided to move into a space in which he could stretch out horizontally.

Gueranger found what he was looking for near Paris's Place de la Bastille – 750 square feet in a group of warehouses at the end of a cul-de-sac. The artist set up a long series of tables in the main space, a former ceramics painting workshop, where he now both lives and works. Only the bedroom is curtained off, and there is no kitchen. "I just eat out all the time," Gueranger said.

*LEFT: The loft is situated in a building of old warehouses and workshops at the end of a cul-de-sac.*

*RIGHT AND BELOW RIGHT: Michel Gueranger's working and living space features a series of large tables as well as modern classical pieces of furniture– chairs by Harry Bertoia and Thonet, and a Le Corbusier chaise. The openwork screen of lacquered wood and the asymmetrical rugs are by the artist.*

# Exhibit space

In 1970, Yves de la Tour d'Auvergne, a sculptor, was already very sensitive to the possibilities of living and working in an unusual space, when he converted a key factory in the Boulevard St. Germain area of Paris into a residential loft for himself and his wife, Soisic. Because the artist, whose works range from small-scale models to monumental pieces, wanted an outdoor area in which he could show his larger sculptures before they went on exhibition or were delivered to collectors, he moved to a street-level loft in the Richard Lenoir area, traditionally the district of restaurant and café equipment manufacturers and wholesalers. The 1,000-square-foot loft had once been a flatware factory.

With the help of his son, Rémy, a young architect, the artist renovated the glass-covered courtyard and transformed the loft into a serene white interior that acts as a background for his sculptural works and his limited-edition pieces of furniture.

*LEFT: In the dining area, the aluminum chairs, glass-and-aluminum table, and sculpture on the wall are all by Yves de la Tour d'Auvergne.*

*ABOVE RIGHT: A glass-covered patio is used as a gallery for the artist's monumental works.*

*RIGHT AND BELOW RIGHT: A low glass table and metal lounge chairs, which were also designed by the artist, furnish the living room.*

LEFT, BELOW LEFT, AND BOTTOM LEFT: *Folded-paper models of the artist's abstract sculptures and furniture are displayed on shelves in the studio.*

RIGHT: *A trestle worktable and rattan armchair face the exterior patio.*

FAR RIGHT: *An experimental sofa in gilded leather and aluminum stands in the studio.*

BELOW RIGHT: *In the living area, a work of painted and corrugated cardboard by Bernard Venet hangs above Yves de la Tour d'Auvergne's metal frame armchairs.*

BELOW FAR RIGHT: *A side chair of textured anodized aluminum is near the dining area.*

# THE OPEN LOFT

Raw lofts interrupted only by columns, and featuring what looks like acres of floor and miles of windows, have from the start sparked the imagination and resources of loft dwellers.

A corner loft is especially prized, because the adjacent rows of windows can allow for light to enter the entire space – even if the loft measures an impressive 5,000 square feet. Top floors capped with skylights are also in demand. But in the classic and most common type of space – 80 feet long and 25 feet wide, a 2,500-square-foot expanse with windows only at one end – daylight can reach the center of the loft only if there are no interior partitions.

Keeping a large space open, an option that attracts people to lofts in the first place, is often a challenge for loft dwellers and designers alike. Kitchens take center stage and are no longer situated behind closed doors; bedrooms are tucked away in convenient corners; and bathrooms are sometimes the only enclosed space in the open loft.

While there is an added sense of communication between members of a family who have learned to respect one another's privacy without the help of architectural barriers, many early open loft aficionados have in the long run resorted to putting up walls to divide their once open space.

*LEFT: The 4,800-square-foot loft of Kipp Trafton of Sointu, a Manhattan design shop, is a soothing, open, Japanese-inspired space that features a 14-foot-long reflecting pool, a skylight, and curved natural-wood platforms.*

## Open expanse

The straightforward, open plan for the 2,400-square-foot New York loft was devised by architect Henry Smith-Miller so that its owner, a painter, would be able to do all the major construction work himself. This meant designating areas for eating, sleeping, and working that would be separated only by freestanding walls or screens, and taking advantage of the structural beams to define the different areas.

The vast expanse features Corinthian columns, Le Corbusier and Rietveld chairs, a table designed by the architect, an antique rug, and a metal sculpture by Robert Murray are the only furnishings in the loft.

*ABOVE: Partition walls define the eating, sleeping, and work areas.*

*LEFT: The loft's natural-wood floor has been waxed and buffed.*

# Converted printing shop

Geneviève Delaunay, a French fashion journalist and stylist, lives with her family in a converted printing shop near Paris's Place de la Nation. The only separate spaces in the loft, designed by Gilles Bouchez, are the bedrooms, both situated on the mezzanine. A wall of glass panels shields the child's room, while the master bedroom was left open and resembles a loggia.

The double fireplace is the pivot of the space, with one side facing the dining area and the other the living and work area.

*ABOVE:* There are no doors on the compact bathroom. Glass windows act as a backsplash to the double sinks, while industrial metal shelving is used for storage.

*ABOVE LEFT:* The tiny kitchen has been situated under the overhanging mezzanine.

*RIGHT:* The painted brick fireplace is at the center of the loft. All the chairs in the space have black frames to contrast with the white interior.

**ABOVE:** A simple hood and exposed duct ventilate the kitchen.

**RIGHT:** A bedroom mezzanine was installed as a second level in the loft. The child's room is enclosed with a series of windows under the eaves.

# Colorful exotica

The loft, 2,150 square feet on Manhattan's lower Fifth Avenue, was a completely open raw space until Maxime de la Falaise was asked to put it together as a pied-à-terre for her European family.

"Eventually, I got the idea of a wedge," she explained of the geometric construction at the center of the space from which radiate the kitchen, bedroom, and dining area. "I don't like things to be too self-explanatory," she added. "Or too neat. I like people to be able to wander about as if they were in a country house that they don't really understand."

Piles of books, plants, and de la Falaise's choice of exotic and colorful textiles add to what she calls "the sense of mystery."

*LEFT: The canopied iron-frame bed is hung with fabrics from Afghanistan.*

*ABOVE RIGHT: The antique armchairs have each been upholstered in a different, colorful textile.*

*RIGHT: On the wall of the bedroom is a painting of Maxime de la Falaise by her father, Oswald Birley, the well-known English portraitist.*

*BELOW RIGHT: The kitchen work unit is open to the living area.*

## Modern art on view

"I like having the loft fairly empty because I don't want it to look like any style in particular," said John Cheim, director of the Robert Miller Gallery and a designer of art books. "I change the way it looks just by changing the paintings around."

Once a glove and purse factory, the 4,300-square-foot Manhattan loft was gutted completely and its floor covered with gray poured acrylic. Cheim opted to construct as few walls as possible, enclosing only the bathroom and installing the kitchen behind a partial wall. There are just a few pieces of furniture – some from the fifties, some in the Empire style–to detract from the huge modern paintings that dominate the large open spaces.

*ABOVE:* The window near the kitchen opens onto a back alley.

*RIGHT:* A column is the only separation between the dining and living areas. The painting on the rear wall is Sales Girls, a 1983 work by David Salle.

*LEFT: Shelves at the end of the long galley kitchen hold a collection of glass and ceramic pieces from antique and junk shops. The rug is African.*

*RIGHT: A 1958 painting, Here I Remember, by Milton Resnick, hangs on the wall near a couch from a factory mail-order catalog.*

*BELOW RIGHT: The living area is furnished with an Empire daybed and small modular slipcovered chairs. The painting on the left is Jedd Garet's 1985 To Rule the World; the one on the right is Andreas Schulze's 1982 Untitled.*

*BOTTOM RIGHT: The bathroom is the only enclosed room. The 1930 drawing is by Gaston Lachaise.*

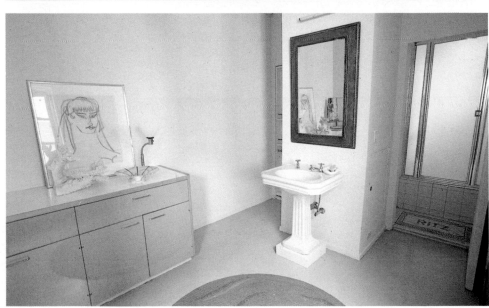

# Unfinished quality

It has been about seven years since Eve Steele, an architectural designer, started working in downtown Los Angeles, an area of warehouses and small factories a few blocks away from what was once the main street of the California city. Now Steele also lives in the neighborhood. Her second-floor loft is located in the former Challenge Dairy Building, a 1926 structure that she converted with a group of investors into 14 residential and two commercial spaces.

The designer spent about $40,000 on renovating the 2,500-square-foot loft, installing new windows and floors, a concrete bathroom, new wiring, and an air-conditioning system. The main living space, which includes a kitchen, has been kept open and sparsely furnished. The bed area is located behind a partition wall and the bathroom is closed off. Exposed concrete columns as well as the space's unfinished quality contribute to the impact of the interior.

*ABOVE: A hole in the roof will eventually be covered with a domed skylight.*

*ABOVE LEFT: The existing concrete column that dominates the open living space was sandblasted.*

*LEFT: The kitchen is adjacent to the living area. New floors were installed throughout the space.*

*ABOVE RIGHT: The small and simply furnished bedroom was situated behind a series of partition walls that let light into the space.*

*RIGHT: The cement tub and sink are in the concrete-walled bathroom.*

## Moving platforms

"Everything must be totally mobile," said Martin Kippenberger, a 26-year-old artist, of the furnishings in his airy 850-square-foot Berlin loft. From its sixth-floor vantage point, the loft has a wide view that ranges over the Kreuzberg area of Berlin and includes East Berlin. Movable screens, a desk on a platform, storage trunks, rolling clothes racks, a portable wardrobe, a futon mattress, and a blue moped are featured objects. Only the paintings are fixed to a single spot.

"Living in a completely open loft allows me to be in charge of the space," Kippenberger explained. "And everything is an expression of my personality."

**ABOVE:** *The loft is located in a converted factory building in Berlin.*

**LEFT:** *Martin Kippenberger is shown in his open loft. Freestanding partitions, a desk on a platform, and a moped are some of the mobile items in the space.*

**LEFT:** *In the bedroom area, clothing is hung on a portable metal rack.*

**RIGHT:** *Only the paintings are fixed to the wall in the minimally furnished loft.*

**BELOW RIGHT:** *The mattress has been set upon a wooden platform. A bookcase is used as a headboard.*

**BELOW:** *An old-fashioned steamer trunk serves as an ad hoc closet.*

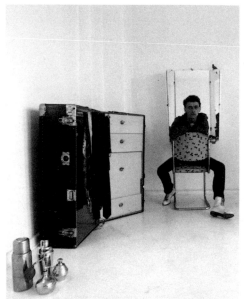

115

# THE DIVIDED LOFT

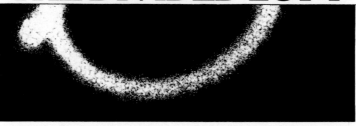

Practical needs led to some of the greatest innovations in loft design. Walls and even separate floors or mezzanine levels have made their appearance as the spaces are custom-tailored to their inhabitants.

The division of the loft was the first step in its gentrification. Loft dwellers–both the pioneers and the new residents–have become older and more settled, and the former industrial spaces are increasingly divided up into living places that have to function for a group of people rather than for a single occupant. The luxury of open, uninterrupted space has given way to more practical considerations of everyday family life.

Separate areas, some partly open to the rest of the space, some completely enclosed, have been created. Low partition walls, greenhouse-like structures, and platforms and furniture arrangements that define areas within a still open expanse have allowed for the systematic carving up of space.

While dividing the loft meant a loss of openness, it also represented an important step in the design evolution of these chameleonlike living places.

*LEFT: In fashion designer Neil Bieff's SoHo loft, architect Henry Smith-Miller designed a wide stairway that goes from the main living space to a small library and catwalk.*

## Color separations

When Neil Bieff, a designer who specializes in evening clothes, moved into his 2,000-square-foot New York SoHo loft, he wanted "to leave its shell intact." Working with architect Henry Smith-Miller, Bieff also sought what he described as "a place like a city desert." To achieve his goal, he had the existing brick walls sandblasted and spent some time finding the right colors. He ended up with a green "originally the color of a eucalyptus leaf, but finally copied from a celadon vase, and a pink that is like the flower of the cactus when it blooms."

The two colors, used on the partition walls and the doors as well as on the centrally placed staircase, contribute to the loft's unusually romantic feeling. Although the furniture often hints at the function of the different areas, there is a great deal of fluidity in the space. And the brick walls, as well as a series of ledges, allow for artworks to be moved and changed at will, without leaving marks on the surfaces.

*LEFT AND BELOW LEFT: The staircase separates the loft's two seating areas—one more formal and furnished with an off-white leather Knoll sofa and a coffee table by Gae Aulenti, the other more informal, with chairs by Le Corbusier.*

*TOP RIGHT AND TOP FAR RIGHT: An antique American Indian basket is displayed on a pedestal by the staircase that leads to the upper floor.*

*RIGHT: A pink wall closes off the dining room, which has a Le Corbusier table and Robert Mallet-Stevens chairs.*

*ABOVE FAR RIGHT: The kitchen, with stainless steel surfaces, has been painted in very dark teal blue.*

*RIGHT AND FAR RIGHT: The master bedroom faces a view of the World Trade Center. The quilt dates from the first half of this century. The oil drawing is by Richard Milani.*

# A house divided

Marianne Held found it one morning – a dilapidated warehouse in a courtyard near Paris's Place de la Bastille – and insisted that her husband, Marc, the designer and architect, come and take a look. "I want it," was Held's immediate reaction. "I realized right away what I could do."

The architect's plan was to preserve as much of the original building as possible, by recycling the bricks and wood. Adding a small garden and a partial second floor, he created a country house in the middle of the city.

A large skylight tops the main living area, which opens onto a lush garden planted with fruit trees and tropical palms. A new brick fireplace is the focal point of the combination living and dining room, while an eat-in kitchen provides a family center.

*LEFT: A wide stairway, as well as a second floor, were included in the conversion of a Parisian warehouse.*

*ABOVE RIGHT: A greenhouse separates the living area from the garden.*

*RIGHT: Bentwood chairs surround the table by the eat-in kitchen. Industrial metal lamps provide lighting.*

*BELOW RIGHT: A sink similar to the kind found in schools is in the entrance.*

*FAR LEFT:* The dining area, with chairs by Harry Bertoia, overlooks the garden.

*LEFT:* An antique claw-footed bathtub has been re-enameled and installed in a corner of the master bedroom.

*BELOW FAR LEFT:* Centered along one wall of the kitchen is a vintage stove.

*BELOW LEFT:* The new fireplace of painted brick provides a focal point for the open living area.

*RIGHT:* Antique linens cover the bed in the tiny, simply furnished bedroom under the eaves.

# Vintage ball court

The 4,000-square-foot loft that belongs to Pieter Estersohn, a young fashion photographer and painter, is located in Manhattan's Flower District and was in 1876 the earliest racket ball court in New York. Since about the turn of the century, it had been used as a factory and was at one time a button workshop before being turned into a residential space 10 years ago. "I still find bits of mother of pearl embedded in the floor," said Estersohn, who recalled that when he first saw the loft, the 14-foot-high ceilings and the unfinished floors and rough walls reminded him of the Fortuny Museum in Venice.

Although the master bedroom is separate, and the guest room up a flight of wooden steps, the rest of the T-shaped space is open, with the kitchen situated at one end and the dining area near the arched windows. "It's a good idea not to forget the salt when you sit down to dinner," Estersohn said.

*ABOVE: The loft building was built in the 1870s as a sports club.*

*TOP RIGHT: The open central portion of the loft is used to display paintings.*

*ABOVE RIGHT: A row of arched windows is one of the best features of the T-shaped space.*

*RIGHT: A long shelf in the dining area is both a bookshelf and buffet.*

*FAR RIGHT: The living room area is furnished with draped sofas and a set of 1925 walnut chairs from France.*

**ABOVE:** *A late 18th-century four-poster bed from England has been placed in the master bedroom.*

**FAR LEFT:** *Mementos are displayed on one of the windowsills.*

**LEFT:** *Part of the bedroom is reflected in the ornate mirror.*

*ABOVE:* Industrial lamps hang in the open kitchen area.

*RIGHT:* A wooden staircase leads up to the mezzanine guest room.

*FAR RIGHT:* The tall ladder is used for building photography sets as well as for changing light bulbs.

# DIVIDING HORIZONTALLY

To most loft dwellers, dividing a large space horizontally is the natural, functional, and logical way. Freestanding cubicles, windowed partition walls, angled corridors, platforms, glass-block walls, and folding or movable screens are some of the elements that have been effective horizontal separations.

But instead of just putting up the needed partitions, many designers have chosen to view the loft division as an opportunity for ingenuity. Some perceive the space as a landscape into which elements can be inserted to suggest a miniature city street, or as a background for interior structures – imagery that echoes the loft's urban esthetic.

*LEFT: Walter Chatham, a New York architect, installed a double colonnade of hollow fluted columns in his loft to define the dining room without enclosing it.*

# Urban landscape

When Michael Tolleson, a young furniture and architectural designer, started thinking about renovating a suite of offices in the 1904 Canadian building, a former consulate in downtown Los Angeles, he saw the space as a "landscape for two buildings."

So Tolleson designed and built two angular freestanding structures, one to house his bedroom, the other to serve as a storage and work area. And because the floor of the 1904 building was not level, Tolleson covered it with gravel and set down lengths of industrial metal grating that function as walkways linking the interior buildings with the minimally furnished living room.

*LEFT: A freestanding building accommodates a small bedroom in a converted office.*

*TOP RIGHT: A chair by Michael Tolleson stands in the entrance foyer.*

*TOP FAR RIGHT: The work surface as well as the storage areas are enclosed by a second interior structure.*

*RIGHT: Only a table and chair are used to furnish the carpeted living room.*

*BELOW RIGHT: The Sheetrock walls of the bedroom have intentionally been left unfinished. The mattress rests directly on the black-and-white-checked floor.*

*BELOW FAR RIGHT: Metal grating, set on gravel, acts as a walkway.*

*ABOVE AND ABOVE RIGHT: In the long entrance corridor, bar stools are positioned at the kitchen pass-through. A narrow door and interior windows open onto the living room area.*

## Interior maze

The basic goal for the design of the 1,100-square-foot loft in Manhattan's TriBeCa was to create separate areas while still maintaining a sense of openness. "Every space had to function in many different ways," said Joan Krevlin, an architect who created the mazelike interior structure with her husband, Harry Kendall, who is also an architect.

A long entrance corridor, set at an angle, provides the illusion of extra space and sets up a circulation route for the loft; below-ceiling-height walls provide for both privacy and storage, and, with the interior windows and door openings, allow for daylight to reach the partially enclosed spaces.

**ABOVE:** *Built-in bookcases allow the bedroom, which is near the living room, to function also as a home office.*

**ABOVE:** *Curtains around the four-poster bed provide coziness and privacy. Architect's flat files supply extra storage.*

## Glass partitions

To reach the open living area of the Paris loft that belongs to Axel le Carpentier, a photographers' and illustrators' agent, one walks past an entrance foyer that is used as an ad hoc garage for bicycles and past a series of glass partitions hung with Venetian blinds that enclose two bedrooms and a bathroom. The few pieces of fifties furniture that define the living room are on a podiumlike platform under the windows.

**TOP:** *The seating area has been defined by a low platform.*

**ABOVE:** *Flea market fifties pieces furnish the dining area.*

**TOP AND ABOVE:** *Glass partitions with Venetian blinds separate the loft bedroom and bathroom spaces.*

**TOP RIGHT:** *The round bathtub on a platform is in a semi-enclosed space off the main corridor.*

# Curved wall

Because she wanted to use the existing bedroom as a studio, Allison Lasley, a painter and interior designer, created a second bedroom in the living room of her small SoHo loft by designing a circular partition wall. The wall, with its glass-block window, divides the living room into an entrance foyer and dining area, and a seating area near the windows. Shades that roll up from the sills take advantage of the light from the tall windows. All the doors, except for those on the closets and bathroom, were removed so that it is possible to see through from one space to another.

*LEFT: A circular wall with a glass-block inset encloses the bedroom.*

*ABOVE RIGHT: The dining area is just inside the front door, by the kitchen.*

*RIGHT: Low seating units are used for the living room area. The wood floors have been bleached.*

*BELOW RIGHT: The bedroom has been furnished with a mattress and shelves built into the round wall.*

## Pattern on pattern

When Donald Billinkoff, a New York architect, needed to divide the Chelsea loft in which he lived with his family, he opted for a series of partitions that turned the 2,400-square-foot space into an intriguing maze.

"There are no doors," Billinkoff explained, "because I didn't know how to hang them myself." Working with Stephen Saitis, a designer, Billinkoff painted each of his new walls in a different color or covered it with a new material. So, while the existing walls of the loft were painted white, the low wall that encloses the small office is covered in white plastic tile; a wall near the master bedroom has been marbleized; a freestanding pinnacled wall by the front door is papered in a chintz pattern; and the kitchen is located behind a double wall of exposed studs.

*LEFT: The ceiling has been exposed in the loft, where a series of textural walls divides the space.*

*LEFT: The kitchen was placed behind open walls of studs.*

*RIGHT: A freestanding arch and a fabric canopy frame the baby's room.*

# Family home

Until about three years ago, the small building in Paris's 14th Arrondissement was used as an office for a group of architects. And although Chantal Hamaide, a home furnishings journalist, and her husband, Thierry Houplain, an advertising art director, wanted to do the renovation work themselves, they asked designer Philippe Boisselier to help convert the space into a family home.

The interior is clean, open, and minimally furnished, with the front entrance opening directly onto the ground-floor bathroom – a large gray-tiled room that is intentionally reminiscent of a public bath.

**ABOVE:** *Le Corbusier chairs surround an extendable table that is separated from the kitchen by a partition wall.*

**OPPOSITE ABOVE LEFT:** *Photographs cover the wall in the work area.*

**OPPOSITE FAR LEFT:** *The small building was once an architect's office.*

**OPPOSITE LEFT:** *A stairway leads directly up to the second floor.*

**FAR LEFT:** *A glass hood is over the stove in the small kitchen.*

**LEFT:** *Pots, pans, and cooking utensils are hung on a metal grid.*

**LEFT:** Rows of bookshelves have been installed under the long second-floor window that overlooks the courtyard.

**BELOW LEFT:** The simply furnished master bedroom is located in what was once a small office.

**BOTTOM LEFT:** The spalike bathroom is right inside the front door on the ground floor of the building.

**RIGHT:** A black leather sofa by Christian Duc is the major piece of furniture in the living room.

**ABOVE:** *Two-way mirror glass has been installed in the angled window.*

**ABOVE RIGHT:** *The bar and storage unit are a miniature version of the façade.*

**RIGHT:** *Brightly painted, the city-street-like construction organizes the different areas of the space.*

# Street scene

Turning an unwieldy 2,100-square-foot space in Manhattan's West Village area into a four-bedroom working and living environment for Melinda Blau and Pamela Serure, partners in a product-development company, was the task given to Michael McDonough, a young New York architect.

"There were also two teenage children, a limited budget, and not much time," said McDonough, who came up with an imaginative and livable scheme based on the angled space. The result was a striking multifaceted architectural divider that looks like a crazy city street but allows the division of the loft into private and public areas. And two-way mirrored panes in the divider windows permit light to enter the ground-floor bedrooms during the day yet provide privacy at night.

## Separate bedroom

A sweeping curved wall of galvanized corrugated metal, a raised banquette, and an interior cubicle lined with glass louvered windows were three of the elements used by Robert Bray and Michael Schaible of Bray-Schaible Design, a New York firm, to create separate areas in the 1,350-square-foot Manhattan loft of Berne Rosen, a young bachelor.

The architectural divisions not only provide for storage, seating, and sleeping but also give the square space a sense of variety. All-white walls and spare classic furniture act as a counterbalance to the changes in flooring materials, from carpeting to limestone, as well as to the various levels that help make the loft feel more spacious.

The focal point of the scheme is the 11-foot-square, centrally placed bedroom, which is enclosed with a series of glass Venetian-blind-like windows of the type often seen on the outside of buildings in the southern United States. Called jalousies, they are especially effective at night, when the lighted bedroom is perceived in the rest of the space as a giant, glowing chandelier.

**ABOVE LEFT:** *A curved wall of corrugated, galvanized steel creates an entrance and also houses a closet.*

**LEFT:** *A raised seating area defines the living room, and a cubicle with louvered windows encloses the bedroom.*

**ABOVE RIGHT:** *Bare white walls and low partitions help retain the open feeling of the space.*

**RIGHT:** *Frosted glass jalousies control light and air in the bedroom.*

## Open and shut space

Having lived in what he called a "conventional apartment complete with antique furniture and curtains," Dennis Goggin wanted a sense of openness when he moved from Europe into a New York loft. "But I also felt I needed something with the potential for privacy," said the banker, who asked architects Laurie Hawkinson and Henry Smith-Miller to design the 1,500-square-foot space.

The architects' solution included a series of sliding doors, screens, and panels, which allow areas of the loft to be closed off yet are flexible enough to be kept open when Goggin is alone.

**ABOVE:** *A Transat chair by Eileen Gray is in the living room area. A pink-painted sliding wall at the rear can close off part of the space.*

**ABOVE LEFT:** *A spotlight creates an egg-shaped design on one of the loft's movable partition walls. The rug is Centimetre by Eileen Gray.*

**ABOVE:** *In contrast to the spacious open living area, the bedroom is intimate and small-scaled.*

**LEFT:** *A series of folding screens set onto an industrial track provide a 20-foot-long movable partition. Glass block separates the living area from the kitchen. The Lota sofa is by Eileen Gray.*

# Multiscreen presentation

Judyth van Amringe, a New York designer of accessories and evening wear, used freestanding screens to provide additional separations in the skylit loft she shares with her husband, Jean de Castella de Delley. A pair of green screens frame the bed; a more translucent white screen stands between the square structural columns of the space.

*TOP: A translucent screen acts as a room divider between the living room area and the more intimate bedroom.*

*ABOVE CENTER: Two antique mirrors have been hung near the bedroom. A basket of lilies stands atop a column.*

*ABOVE LEFT: The tall windows in the living area have been left uncovered. Seating is provided by a leather sofa and a Transat chair by Eileen Gray with a red lacquered frame.*

*ABOVE: The bed covered in antique linens and small night table are behind a screen that doubles as a headboard.*

**LEFT:** Translucent plastic panels found on the street have been made into a screen that provides privacy for an at-home gym area in John Cheim's New York loft.

**ABOVE:** A multipanel screen of chipboard, slate, and sprayed bronze, by French designer Olivier Gagnère, acts as a space divider in a 4,000-square-foot Manhattan Chelsea loft.

# DIVIDING VERTICALLY

Sleeping lofts, which took advantage of an expanse's double-height ceilings, were among the first and least ambitious of the early loft living solutions. Mezzanine floors that could nearly double the square footage of a space, and dramatic stairways connecting separate floors or offering access to rooftops, were also important in loft renovations and in many instances became the central design element of the newly converted space.

Loft dwellers were usually unwilling to give up the sense of openness they prized so dearly. So, they often tried to keep the best of both worlds, installing partial second floors that provided private spaces such as bedrooms and bathrooms and keeping the main living area open and able to be seen to dramatic advantage from above.

*LEFT: A Corinthian cast-iron column bisects a mezzanine in the Doners' New York loft.*

# Nature study

When Michele Oka Doner, a sculptor, moved to New York with her husband, Fred, and two teenage sons, she was determined to live in a loft that was "filled with light." After an exhaustive search, she found a 5,000-square-foot two-level space in SoHo that had been renovated by Michael S. Wu, a young architect. "All we needed to do was adapt it to family life," Doner explained. "We created a few private spaces – a small library downstairs, and a series of bedrooms on the mezzanine."

Doner also set up her studio in a corner of the ground-floor space and furnished the loft with the family's collections of naturalist objects as well as a number of unusual antiques and some furniture the artist had designed herself. "I have always been able to make the things I needed," she said.

*ABOVE:* A zigzagging stair leads to the upper floor.

*RIGHT:* The balcony and mezzanine overlook the main living area. Unusually decorative cast-iron columns are ringed with their original radiators.

LEFT: *In the kitchen area, the double sink and the stove have been built into a freestanding unit. The refrigerator is topped with a peaked roof to give it the appearance of a small building.*

RIGHT: *The mezzanine level, with its curved balcony, was added to the space.*

BELOW RIGHT: *One end of the main living space is used as a work area. The birch tables are by the artist.*

BOTTOM RIGHT: *The sculptor's studio is located near the living room. Pieces of her shell- and coral-inspired works sit on high tables.*

# Little yellow house

Faced with the renovation of a 16-foot-wide, 50-foot-long, high-ceilinged loft in an old burglar alarm factory, Chicago-based architect Kenneth Schroeder decided to build a vertical houselike structure complete with a pitched roof, a skylight, windowlike openings, a steep carpeted stair, and Doric columns.

By painting the 12-foot-square tower bright yellow and setting it at an angle to the walls of the rectilinear space, Schroeder created not only a conversation piece but also a functional series of nooks that accommodate a study and a place to hang a hammock.

*LEFT AND BELOW LEFT: The interior structure provides a vertical focus for the 50-foot-long loft as well as a series of private spaces that includes a second-floor study stories.*

*RIGHT: A stairway allows access to the upper floor of the tower. Windowlike openings and Doric columns are some of the details of the yellow building.*

## Converted school

By removing the tin ceiling above a loft space on the top floor of a 200-year-old schoolhouse in Brooklyn Heights, New York, Siris/Coombs Architects was able to expose the trussed-wood roof structure and create a two-level residence.

A bridge landing, or mezzanine, divides the loft vertically; three bedrooms were installed between the trusses. A study/playroom is up a small ladder from the mezzanine, where openings allow for a view of the spacious living area below. A wide carpeted stairway with steel-tube railings links the two main floors.

*ABOVE AND LEFT: The conversion of a loft in an old Brooklyn schoolhouse included raising the roof and installing a second floor.*

# Rooftop suite

"A staircase as big as possible" was one of Bénédicte Siroux's requirements when she and Maurizio Benadon, a real estate developer, converted a top-floor New York loft into a duplex living space. Siroux, a furniture importer, planned the space with interior designer Kevin Walz, adding a master bedroom suite on the roof of the Chelsea building.

The dramatic, surrealistic, and bannisterless stair links the top floor to the 2,500-square-foot floor below. White walls, diaphanous white draperies, pale gray-stained floors, tall columns, and diffuse light emphasize the loft's neoclassical look.

*LEFT: An imposing open stair is at the center of the duplex loft.*

*RIGHT: On the lower floor, a centrally situated column defines the living room. The windows are draped with white cotton gauze that diffuses the light.*

*BELOW RIGHT: In the living room, the sofa is a reproduction of a Jean-Michel Frank design and the unframed paintings are by the French artist Guillain Siroux, Bénédicte Siroux's father.*

ABOVE: *A fanciful wrought-iron dressing table stool stands by the window in the second-floor master bedroom.*

ABOVE: *White gauze draperies frame the bed, over which hangs a painting by Guillain Siroux. A large bandbox doubles as a low table.*

RIGHT: *The dining room area has been located between the kitchen and the stair. The wrought-iron table and chairs came from an antique shop. The painting on the wall is by Mattia Bonetti, a French artist and furniture designer.*

## Structural essentials

Malcolm and Mimi MacDougall – he's an advertising executive and she's a partner in a housewares shop – wanted a city feeling in their New York loft situated in the Gainsborough Studios, a landmark building that overlooks Central Park. This gave Valerie Boom, an architect with Redroof Design, the impetus to strip the double-height space down to its structural essentials.

The loft's steel support beam was painted bright blue, along with the metal stair and the mezzanine railings. The stark white walls, shiny black-painted wood floors, and use of concrete block, wire glass, and brick emphasize the urban esthetic.

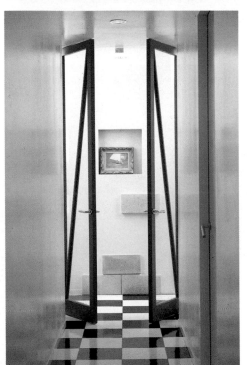

*TOP:* Bookcases allow the mezzanine to be used as a library.

*ABOVE:* Wire glass doors open onto the master bedroom wing.

*ABOVE: A blue-painted metal stairway leads to the upper level of the loft.*

# River view

According to Juan Montoya, a New York interior designer, the 2,800-square-foot loft that overlooked the Hudson River was too wide open. "I felt I had to create a more intimate feeling," he explained of the overscale furniture, carpeting, wood detailing around the fireplace, beige-pink walls, and dining area sheltered by the bedroom mezzanine.

*TOP:* The huge window at one end of the loft overlooks the piers.

*ABOVE:* The bedrooms are situated on the mezzanine.

*RIGHT:* The carpeted living room area is focused around the fireplace and furnished with low, black leather-covered sofas.

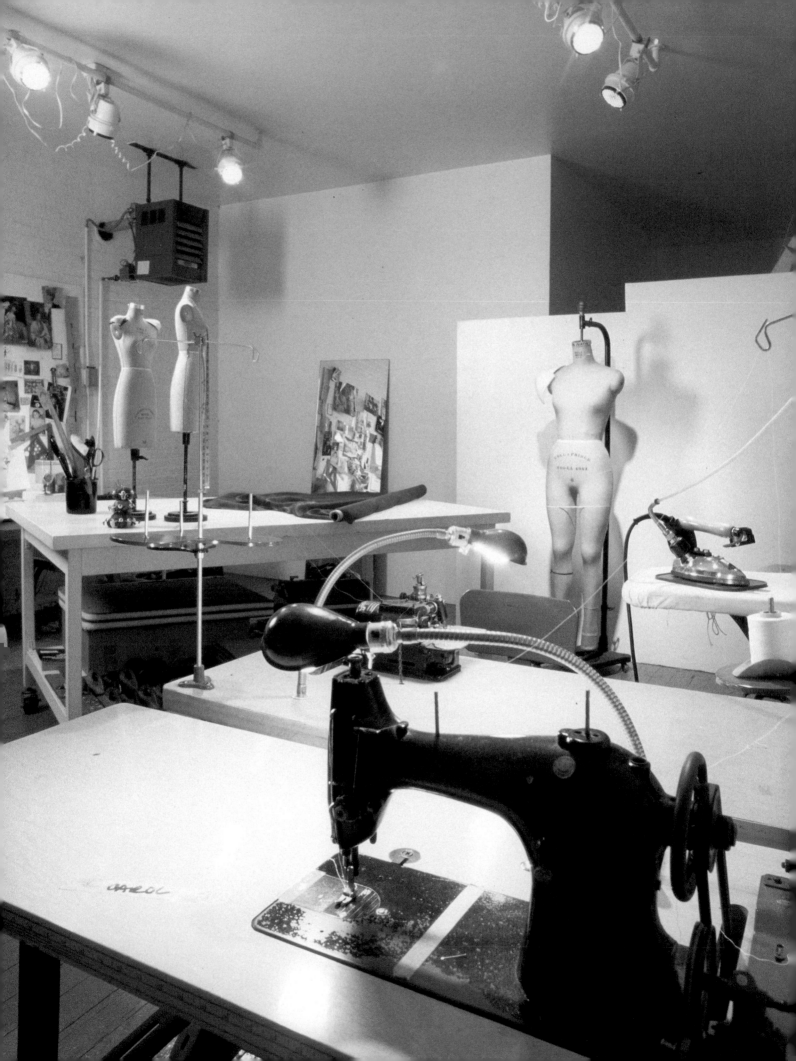

# LIVING AND WORKING

Although there have always been a number of people who incorporate offices, studios, and workrooms into their homes, lofts have allowed for a freer, more ambitious, and often less segregated working and living situation. The scale and freedom of the loft space–the opportunity to organize the environment around particular needs–makes it adaptable to nearly any profession.

While artists were the first to take advantage of lofts to integrate their studios and living places, photographers, fashion designers, architects, lawyers, accountants, and writers have quickly followed suit. Some have chosen to divide the lofts structurally in order to create a separation between the professional and private areas; others prefer to maintain an open expanse and circulation. Many are also able to use part of the loft space as a showroom or gallery.

The trompe l'oeil walls of a photographer's living space double as an exotic background for fashion shootings; the table and chairs in the loft of a vintage furniture dealer are for sale to clients; and it is not unknown for designers to sit down to dinner at their drafting tables.

*LEFT: Dressmakers' mannequins, long wooden tables, and sewing machines fill the work area of fashion designer Carol Fertig's Lower Manhattan loft.*

## Classical colonnade

Claude Mougin, a French fashion photographer, knew that he needed a large place in which he could both work and live with his wife, Mae, and two daughters, Solange and Zoé. The 4,800-square-foot loft in Manhattan's Chelsea area, with its 14 south-facing windows, afforded enough raw space to be turned into a studio and office, as well as providing a centrally situated kitchen and dining room and a bedroom wing.

Working with Robert M. Lohman, an interior designer, and Pierre Hitier, an artist and muralist, Mougin chose to create an interior that would be his own interpretation of the ruins of Pompeii and Rome. A colonnade of plump columns, trompe l'oeil painted walls, and a columned and pedimented four-poster bed symbolize the effective mix of classicism with modern fantasy. "What I wanted to convey was a feeling of nostalgia, a romantic view of the past," Mougin said.

*ABOVE: The loft's marbleized walls are sometimes used as a backdrop for photographic sessions.*

*RIGHT: The classical colonnade is the most important design element of the renovated space.*

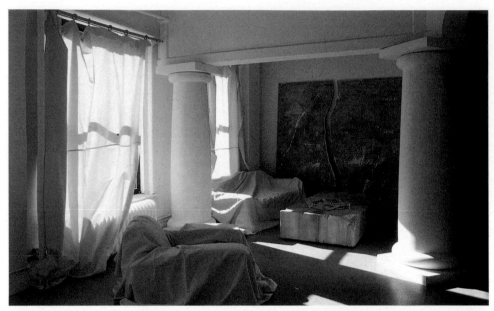

*LEFT: In the living room area, a wall has been painted in trompe l'oeil stone and the furniture is loosely draped.*

*BELOW LEFT: The dining room walls are also covered with a faux stone design. New bleached-wood chairs surround a granite-top table. A pair of monumental columns frame the entrance to the bedroom corridor.*

*BOTTOM LEFT: Makeup mirrors and photographic lights are in the area of the loft designated as a studio.*

*RIGHT: The pedimented and columned bed was assembled from salvaged architectural remnants.*

# Caterer's kitchen

A commercial kitchen that would not look too sterile, a living room that could be rented out for both large and small parties, and an office that could accommodate a growing computer service company were the three requisites that a young New York couple gave Matthew Gottsegen when they asked him to design their loft. She is a cook and caterer, he a computer expert, and they both wanted to live and work in one space.

The high-tech feeling of the stainless steel kitchen outfitted with professional equipment was softened by the use of pink and beige tile and the caterer's personal collection of antique bowls and platters. The living room was sparsely furnished with movable pieces that can be easily shifted around when rented tables and chairs are brought in or when the floor needs to be cleared for dancing.

*LEFT: Bowls and platters are kept on open shelves in the caterer's kitchen.*

*ABOVE RIGHT: The professional kitchen is adjacent to the loft's living area, which is also used for parties.*

*RIGHT: Plastic sheeting covers the off-white cotton sofas to protect them from city dirt.*

*BELOW RIGHT: A separate room off the foyer accommodates the computer service business.*

## Plant life

Catherine Willis is a young conceptual artist and botanist who has based her work on exploiting the scents of different plants in the pursuit of art and fantasy rather than science.

In the heart of Paris's historic Marais district, behind a garage, the loft is Willis's experimental workshop. Within a minimally furnished Japanese-inspired interior, the artist creates her ephemeral carpets of petals and plants that are meant to last only until they are swept away by a broom.

*LEFT: Plant specimens from all over the world are neatly stored in cubicles.*

*RIGHT: Catherine Willis creates one of her naturalistic pieces.*

*BELOW RIGHT: Scented petals are sewn into the hem of the kimono, which is also one of the artist's works. A series of counter-balanced industrial lamps hangs from the ceiling.*

*BELOW: The round rug is made up of dried leaves and petals.*

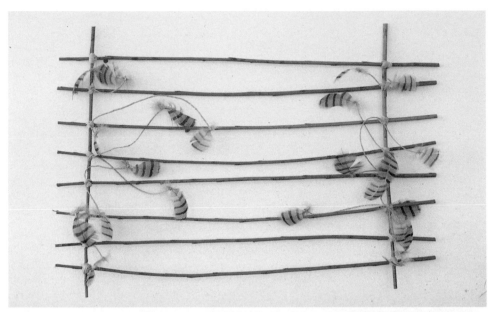

LEFT, BELOW LEFT, AND BOTTOM
LEFT: *Feathers delicately strung on
wooden sticks, plant specimens dried in
a notebook, and strips of cloth that
experiment with color are part of the
artist's botanical collection.*

RIGHT AND BELOW RIGHT: *Bowls and
baskets filled with a variety of plants and
herbs are not only meant to be
decorative but are also valued for their
unusual scents.*

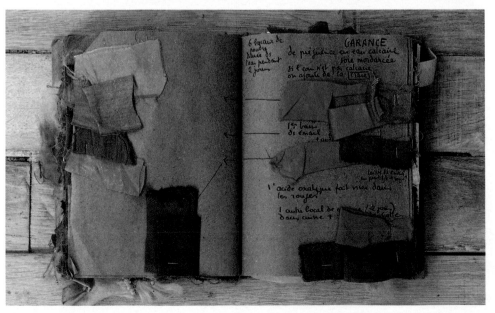

186

# High-tech house

It took Nancy and Claude Kent over a year to plan the renovation of the small downtown Los Angeles warehouse into a carpentry workshop, artist's studio, and living space.

The Kents, who own Industrial Revolution, two high-tech home furnishings stores, had the 6,400-square-foot structure reinforced and added a new roof without changing the character of the building. "The idea was to keep the interior pretty rough," Nancy Kent said of the ground floor of the two-story building, which features a sandblasted wood ceiling, brick walls, exposed ductwork, and new wood floors.

The workshop and studio, as well as a large room for displaying paintings and a spacious main living area, are all contained on the ground floor. A black metal stair leads to a 550-square-foot studio apartment on the second floor that includes a living and sleeping space, bathroom, and open galley kitchen. "It's a small room," Nancy Kent explained, "so we wanted to keep everything really clean and spare." To further increase the feeling of spaciousness, the walls were painted white and the furniture is low and small-scaled.

*ABOVE:* The exterior of the warehouse features a glass-block window that provides privacy while allowing light into the interior.

*ABOVE LEFT:* Architect's flat-file cabinets line one wall of the ground-floor space that is used as a gallery.

*ABOVE RIGHT:* The artist's studio and woodworking shop are situated on the ground floor, with easy access to the loading docks for delivery of materials.

*LEFT AND RIGHT:* The living and dining areas on the ground floor are minimally furnished. The new wood floors have been bleached, stained, and waxed.

**TOP:** *A bed that doubles as a couch is the only large piece of furniture in the room. The walls are white and the floors covered in industrial carpeting.*

**ABOVE CENTER:** *Black granite-topped cabinets line the open kitchen.*

**ABOVE:** *The bathroom sink unit matches the kitchen cabinets.*

**RIGHT:** *On the second floor, there is a combination living room, bedroom, and gallery kitchen.*

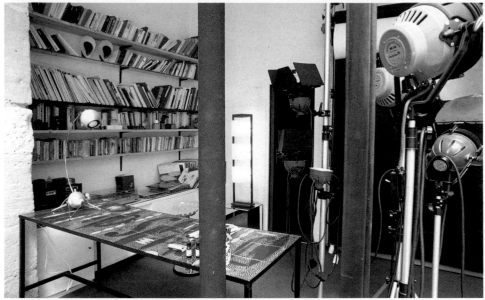

# Fifties revival

The two-story house at the end of a passageway in Paris's Faubourg St. Antoine, an area of woodworking shops since the 17th century, was converted by Jean Philippe Glezes into a residence and photographer's studio. The new interior – two floors connected by a small plant-lined stairway – incorporates such modern materials as metal railings and struts and glass block. Contrasting with the clean shell of the house is its occupant's colorful collection of fifties rugs, furniture, and lighting as well as his Art Deco ceramics and glass.

*ABOVE: The loft is actually a small two-story house.*

*TOP LEFT: In the living area, an Italian sofa by Paolo Deganello is combined with fifties pieces.*

*ABOVE LEFT: Photographer's lighting stands near a fifties ceramic-topped table in the studio.*

*LEFT: Near the kitchen, a folding table has integrated chairs that are pulled out for dining.*

*RIGHT: The living area faces the staircase that leads to the upper floor.*

**ABOVE LEFT:** *The combination bedroom and bathroom is under the eaves.*

**LEFT:** *A tall glass-block window lets light into the ground floor.*

**ABOVE:** *A sloping glass roof creates a plant-filled atrium.*

**ABOVE LEFT:** *The organically shaped bathtub is enclosed with mosaic tile laid in a wavelike pattern.*

## Model home

The 2,000-square-foot New York loft now lived in by Howard Read, an art dealer with the Robert Miller Gallery, and Katia Ramsey, a fashion stylist, was once a warehouse for a shoe factory.

The loft is organized along a corridor that is used as a display space for photographs, with a windowed kitchen at one end and a living room and work area at the other. Particularly useful is the fact that the stylist can turn the loft into a spacious work environment, taking advantage of the large living area for fittings and modeling sessions during the day.

*ABOVE: The narrow hallway doubles as a photograph gallery.*

*LEFT: The living area, with its high-gloss wood floors, has been furnished with a sofa by Paul T. Frankl and a round drum table that came from a Bonwit Teller department store display.*

**ABOVE:** *A dermatology lamp, found on the street, stands by the desk in the work area. The sticks on the bookcase came from the country. Flat files under the desk provide extra storage for photographs and artworks.*

**ABOVE:** *Chairs from a Horn & Hardart Automat surround a table made from a coat rack in the eat-in kitchen. Katia Ramsey created the sculptural still-life in the niche.*

**RIGHT:** *The freestanding 1950 sculpture is by Louise Bourgeois. Leaning against the wall is a 19th-century Italian architectural photograph.*

## Warehouse on the Thames

When Sam Sprague first moved into the old stone warehouse building that overlooks London's Thames River, he knocked down walls, sanded floors, did electrical work, and installed a bathroom and kitchen. The English furniture designer, modelmaker, and craftsman wanted to convert the 2,500-square-foot space into a combination design office, metal, plastic, and wood workshop, and open living area.

One of the most unusual features of the design studio space is its completely white-tiled walls. "I've tried to find out why all the walls were tiled," Sprague said. "I can only suspect that it had something to do with using the place to store food and needing to wash it down. Sometimes, it just feels like I'm living in a men's room."

*ABOVE LEFT, LEFT, AND BELOW LEFT: The warehouse building, with windows painted bright red on the exterior, is situated on the Thames.*

*RIGHT AND BELOW RIGHT: Original white tiles line the walls of the open work and living areas.*

*BELOW: The bookcase and storage units are some of the pieces made in the loft.*

## Industrial design

Although Helena Uglow, an English industrial designer, reserved a small area of the Lower Manhattan loft in which she has lived for the past eight years only for "dirty work"—making plaster, clay, and wood models—she uses the rest of the space to create her works in metal, plastic, and glass.

"I design useful objects that I hope are beautiful," Uglow said. "When I make things for the kitchen, such as kettles, saucepans, and serving platters, I try them out in the dishwasher, then display them on the counter tops." In the living area, she uses the walls for designing textiles. "That's where I stretch a piece of paper and draw on it," she explained.

The corner loft, with its 10 windows, boasts an open view of the Hudson River and New Jersey. "The changes in weather and light are incredible," Uglow added. "It's rather like living on board a ship or out-of-doors in the middle of the city."

*ABOVE: Beyond the desk are the L-shaped studio and "dirty work" area.*

*LEFT: White paint has been used for the floors, walls, and ceiling of the main living area of the loft.*

*LEFT:* The manually operated freight elevator opens directly into the loft.

*LEFT:* A few of the designer's one-of-a-kind ceramics are displayed on the exposed-iron radiator.

*LEFT:* Canvas folding director's chairs surround the dining room table.

*RIGHT: A large piece of paper, pinned to the wall, is meant to be used to design a new textile pattern.*

*RIGHT: The kitchen is open to the main living space. The counter serves as a surface for showing off cookware and serving pieces.*

*RIGHT: The monastic and simply furnished bedroom includes an antique settle brought from England. The windowsill doubles as a bedside table.*

## Furniture showroom

The 19th-century building where Mara Cremniter and François Laffanour have their 1,500-square-foot loft, like many other loft buildings near Paris's Place de la Bastille, once housed the small workshops of furniture craftsmen and tailors. The couple, who are partners in Down Town, a gallery and shop on the Rue de Seine specializing in fifties and sixties furniture, also use their home as an ad hoc showroom. "But only by appointment," Cremniter said.

The open space, which has simply been cleaned up and repainted, acts as a backdrop for the furniture by well-known architects and designers of the last three decades. "We like the exuberance of the fifties," Cremniter said. "And we also like lots of things from the sixties. But often, we have to realize that the objects we've been living with might not be there for long."

**LEFT:** *Jean Prouvé, the French architect, designed the dining room table. The chairs are by Werner Panton. A 1970s sculpture by Yannis Gaitis lines the wall.*

**RIGHT:** *The open expanse of the loft allows for a flexible placement of furniture. Two white 1960s chairs by the Italian architect Joe Colombo are between the living and dining areas.*

**RIGHT:** *A yellow plush covered sofa by Jean Royère, a French interior decorator, is called L'Ours Polaire and was designed in 1950. Maurice Calca, a French designer, created the white plastic Leleu desk in 1960; the floor-to-ceiling bookshelves by Suzanne Vandamme, a French designer, also date from that year.*

# THE LOFT IN DETAIL

One of the most distinctive aspects and determining elements of any loft is the overscale features of the space. Twelve-foot-high ceilings, huge stretches of cement or solid wood floors, 40-foot-long sandblasted brick walls, and rhythmic rows of arched windows are often standard rather than extraordinary loft attributes.

Dealing with these elements—as well as unusual radiators and pipes, columns, and beams—has inspired designers and architects to come up with practical and ingenious solutions. But often, and again because of the scale of many of the lofts, window coverings, doors, and partition walls, for example, have had to be custom-made.

Floor-to-ceiling metal doors with sandblasted glass panels provide privacy without blocking out natural light; window shades that pull up from the bottom of the sill also allow for a view of the sky or rooftops without closing off the window completely. Canvas screens as room dividers, blinds made from nylon sails, and glass-block interior windows are other materials that seem to work particularly well in the loft environment.

*LEFT: A black door, tiled foyer, and clerestory grid mark the entrance to the upstairs loft in a 1902 New York carriage house converted by Peter Coan of Redroof Design.*

**LEFT:** The angled ceiling and walls exaggerate the perspective and create a dramatic view of an elevator door that opens directly into a Manhattan Chelsea loft by Walter Chatham.

**RIGHT:** A double-height ceiling in Howard Read and Katia Ramsey's New York loft allowed for the installation of a tall closet with painted doors that each open separately.

**FAR RIGHT:** In a New York loft by Laura Bohn and Joseph Lembo, a floor-to-ceiling pivoting door opens onto the master bedroom.

**BELOW RIGHT:** Walter Chatham set a two-part door that leads into a small kitchen a few inches away from the wall in a Chelsea loft.

**FAR RIGHT:** Sandblasted glass in a black steel frame was used by Walter Chatham for a floor-to-ceiling door in a Manhattan loft.

**BOTTOM RIGHT:** A canvas roll-down shade acts as a door in photographer Jan Staller's TriBeCa loft.

**BOTTOM FAR RIGHT:** The front door of Eve Steele's Los Angeles loft is part of a floor-to-ceiling metal grid construction.

**LEFT:** *Nylon mesh blinds that roll up from the bottom of the windows were installed by designer Laura Bohn in her New York loft.*

**BELOW LEFT:** *Venetian blinds cover the openings under the sloping glass window in a New York loft by Allen Scruggs and Douglas Myers.*

**RIGHT:** *A huge sail of parachute silk covers the double row of windows in the 28-foot-high SoHo loft of Antonio Morello and Donato Savoie. The fabric can be adjusted to three positions, and not only diffuses the light but also acts as a dramatic design element in the minimally furnished space.*

# THE LOFT INFLUENCE

While lofts were originally sought out by those who needed large spaces and were willing to live in unconventional and marginal areas of the city, the style of living they represent soon came to appeal to many people who prefer the amenities of established residential neighborhoods. And although most apartments are not of a comparable scale, lofts have engendered new concepts of space that have become an important factor in their redesign.

Kitchens that open directly onto the main living area, rooms defined only by the placement of furniture, flexible partitions, and in general, a more open and communicative series of spaces, are features of brownstones and apartments that seem to have come directly from lofts.

Unusual materials also made their way into the more traditional buildings; industrial or commercial carpeting—often used to cover huge expanses of office floors and, in their muted tones and textures, synonymous with a minimal esthetic—are now interior design staples, along with bare windows and stainless steel kitchen counters.

Even the restaurant stove, a loft prerequisite, has been adopted by apartment dwellers. Most dramatic, though, are the projects that start out from scratch, conceived and built to resemble lofts. A sculptor's suburban metal house is loftlike in its expanse and openness; a beach house, with an interior accented by bright red metal struts and columns, is an example of the loft esthetic in all of its enthusiasm. Far from the industrial neighborhood that inspired it, the house is now a loft with ocean view.

*LEFT: The late interior designer Doug Frank opened up the space in a narrow Manhattan brownstone apartment and installed low partitions to create the feeling of a small loft.*

# Space capsules

"This place was both influenced by and a reaction against the loft in which I used to live," said Deyan Sudjic, a London-based journalist. "The loft I had was dark. This is the opposite."

Sudjic's light-filled apartment, in the Little Venice area of London, is made up of a single floor of two adjoining 1840's town houses. Jan Kaplicky, in London, and David Nixon, in Los Angeles, two architects in the transatlantic firm Future Systems, devised the space-age interior. "I wanted it to be white, clean, and sunny," Sudjic recalled. Kaplicky responded by scooping out everything from the warren of rooms and installing a series of platforms that don't touch the exterior shell of the apartment. A huge keyhole-shaped opening was made in the three-foot-thick wall that separated the two apartments and now creates a passageway between the dining room and the living room.

"The platforms helped identify the areas by defining individual spaces within a whole," Sudjic said. "Living in a loft is always sort of temporary, and I like more support."

*ABOVE: The apartment spans two 1840 town houses.*

*TOP LEFT AND ABOVE LEFT: Both the dining room and the bedroom have floors of aluminum sheeting. Built-in electrical conduits allow the lamps to be plugged directly into the floor.*

*LEFT: In the bathroom, the side panels have been removed from a standard bathtub. The sink and toilet are cantilevered out from an aluminum-paneled wall and the floor is covered in linoleum.*

*RIGHT: The keyhole-shaped opening leads to the living room.*

**ABOVE AND LEFT:** *The kitchen has been located on a raised aluminum-covered platform that has been edged in neoprene rubber. The appliances are all contained within a built-in work unit. Simple open metal shelves hold cooking and eating utensils.*

## Metalwork

After giving up looking for a place in Manhattan in which he could both live and work, Robert Perless, a sculptor, and his wife, Ellen, an advertising executive, decided to build their own version of a modern, open loft on a wooded six-acre site in Greenwich, Connecticut.

With the help of John Ciardullo, a New York-based architect and structural engineer, the couple created a 130-foot-long, 6,500-square-foot building with both living quarters and a huge studio.

Using the same materials that Perless works with in his sculpture, they devised a framework made of steel and exterior walls of aluminum paneling, similar to that on New York's Citicorp Building.

The main interior space, which had to be large enough to hang one of Perless's monumental steel mobiles, boasts 25-foot-high ceilings. The glass-walled master bedroom is cantilevered over the minimally furnished living area.

In spite of its awesome size, the couple thinks of their home as "only a three-bedroom house." And to prove that he was still a city boy at heart, the sculptor forgot to plan for a garage. "I still have to park outside," Perless said.

*ABOVE: A sleek white fireplace stands at the center of the dramatic open loftlike main living space.*

*LEFT: Robert Perless's 1982* Air Planes/ White *hangs from the 25-foot-high ceiling. The space is furnished with pieces by Miës van der Rohe and Breuer, and the steps and platforms are covered with industrial carpeting.*

# Uptown adaptation

Designed for a New York couple who had considered moving to a loft but decided to stay in the Upper East Side neighborhood, the two-bedroom apartment, the only one on the floor, was renovated so as to provide maximum flexibility without destroying the small scale of the rooms. Yann Weymouth of Redroof Design created a new traffic pattern for the 1,100-square-foot space, taking down most of the walls. The kitchen is now open to the dining room and a sliding door has been installed between the second bedroom and the living room. Perforated metal radiator covers, used throughout to unify the spaces visually, and stainless steel kitchen units are the only built-in elements in the apartment.

*ABOVE LEFT: A Lota sofa by Eileen Gray, coffee tables by Florence Knoll, and a pair of chairs by Pierre Jeanneret furnish the living room.*

*LEFT: The pantry has been opened up to the dining room. Decorative bowls, glassware, and ceramics are displayed on a metal shelving unit above a stainless steel kitchen sink.*

*BELOW LEFT: A pale pink sliding door separates the guest bedroom from the living room. The closet doors are covered in marbleized plastic laminate.*

*RIGHT: A radiator cover of perforated metal lines the wall under the window in the living room. The wrought-iron plant stand in the corner is by the French architect Pierre Chareau.*

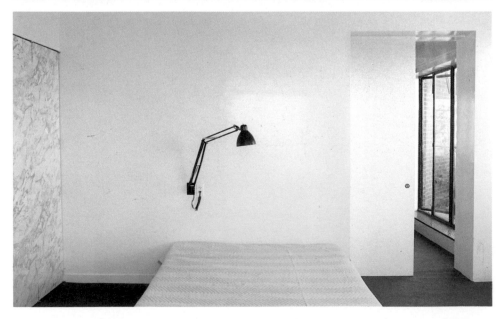

# Grid pattern

The structural steel beams, painted gray, and the pivoting panels, colored pink, are the two basic organizational elements in the conversion of a traditional Milanese apartment, by Alberto Gardino, into a flexible, open-plan combination office and home.

A floor-to-ceiling grid screen, a glass wall, and a series of staircases leading to an upper floor not only differentiate the living, dining, kitchen, and work areas but also give the multilevel interior a sense of being a small-scaled cityscape.

Classical modern furniture by Le Corbusier and Breuer and the industrial lighting and metal storage units create a sophisticated and dramatically serene interior.

*TOP AND ABOVE: A pivoting pink panel allows for the living room to be separated from or open to an office work area.*

*RIGHT: The structural beam over the main living space is the only inflexible element of the interior.*

*RIGHT:* The dining room table and chairs by Le Corbusier are set in front of a see-through grid that serves as a partition from the kitchen.

*RIGHT:* An industrial lighting fixture hangs above the freestanding work island in the kitchen.

**LEFT:** *The round form in the bedroom encloses a shower.*

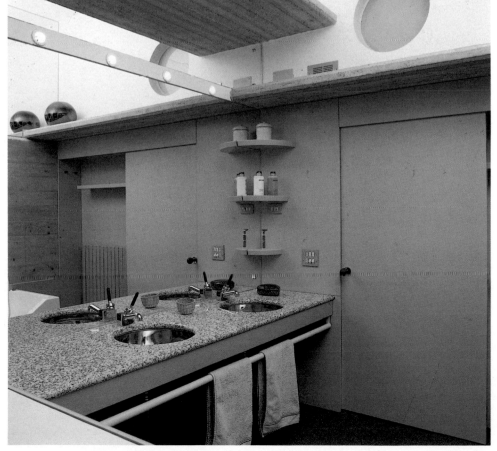

**LEFT:** *In the bathroom, the sinks are set into a granite counter. The walls are finished in gray lacquered polyester.*

# Ocean-view loft

When Michael Kooper, a consultant in the health insurance business, decided to build on a piece of oceanfront property on Long Island, New York, he knew that what he wanted was to have a big open loft on the beach. Kooper and his wife, Elisabeth, worked with David Enock, the president of Eisenman & Enock, a Manhattan advertising agency, designers Robin Drake and Neal Mayer, and architects Donald and Liisa Sclare to design the house.

"The main idea was to be able to see the ocean," said Enock, who raised the house on its site and provided for seating that is parallel to the dunes and allows an uninterrupted view of the beach. Red steel beams span the airy and open 3,000-square-foot main living space; the other areas are separated from one another only by a series of canvas partitions hung on metal screens. A restaurant kitchen with a delicatessen refrigerator case and commercial ice makers, a separate cooking kitchen, back-to-back bathroom sinks, beds on casters, sleeping lofts for extra guests, exercise equipment, and what is maybe the most luxurious element of all in a weekend place, a well-equipped and convenient laundry room, are features of the loftlike house.

*ABOVE RIGHT: Wide steps lead up to the entrance to the beach house.*

*RIGHT: The stainless steel serving kitchen features a delicatessen counter and has been dramatically positioned in the open main living space.*

*RIGHT: A high kitchen counter is used for dining.*

*FAR RIGHT: Near the front door, a sleeping loft accommodates extra weekend guests.*

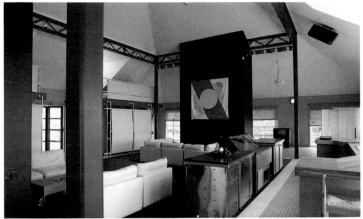

**TOP:** *The exposed structural steel beams have been painted bright red.*

**ABOVE:** *Towels hang on hooks near the laundry area, which is situated near the living space.*

**LEFT:** *The floor throughout the house is covered with two-inch-square ceramic tiles. Carpeting has been provided for the area near the fireplace.*

**ABOVE:** *A canvas and tubular steel screen separates one of the bedroom areas from the cooking kitchen.*

**RIGHT:** *Stereo speakers and hardware-less cabinets have been set into the fireplace, which also acts as a partition wall between one of the bedroom areas and the main living space.*

**ABOVE:** The master bathroom, with its sunken tub and freestanding sink, is open and adjacent to the bedroom area. A ceiling fan cools the space, and heating vents have been installed flush in the tiled floor.

**LEFT:** The lighting fixtures along the perimeter walls come from a marine supply store. The bed, with its tubular steel frame, as well as the small side tables, are on casters.

***ABOVE:*** *Iris Kaplan, a painter, had Scott Bromley and Robin Jacobsen design a glass-topped loft-like artist's studio for her off the living room of her Park Avenue apartment in New York City.*

# PLANS AND ISOMETRICS

Once a loft has been renovated, it is difficult to tell the imaginative planning and complicated construction involved in the finished space. Plans and isometric drawings situate the different areas and give an overall sense of the design process.

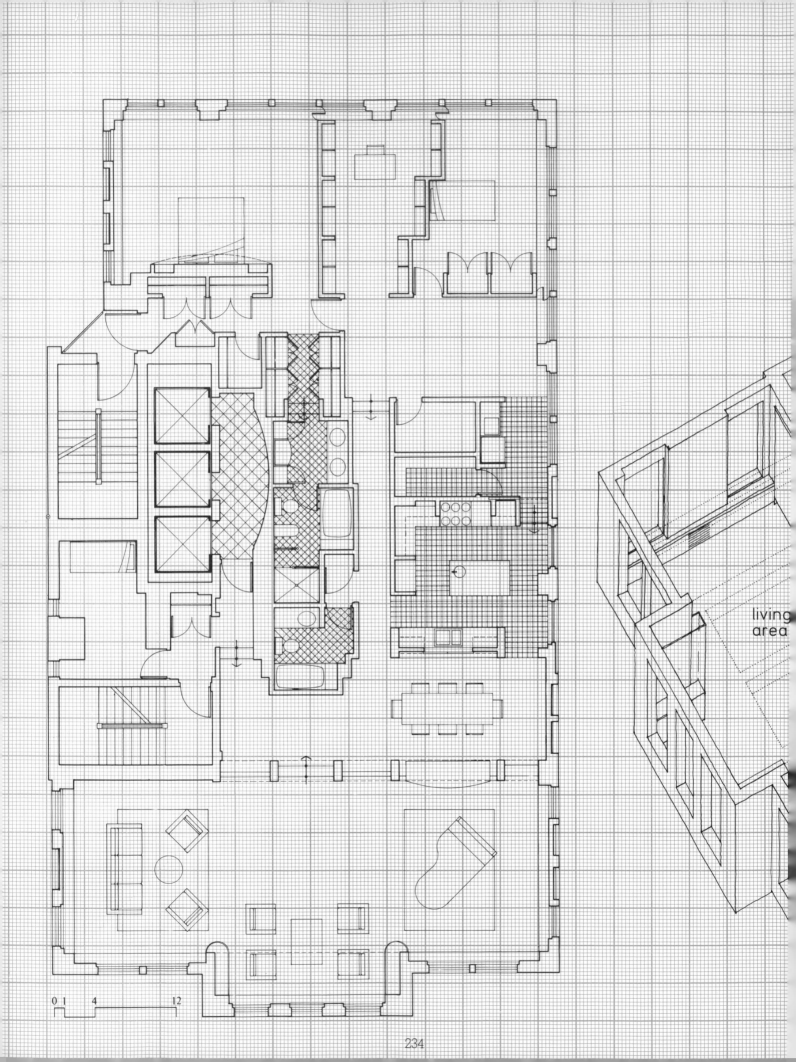

living
area

0 1    4          12

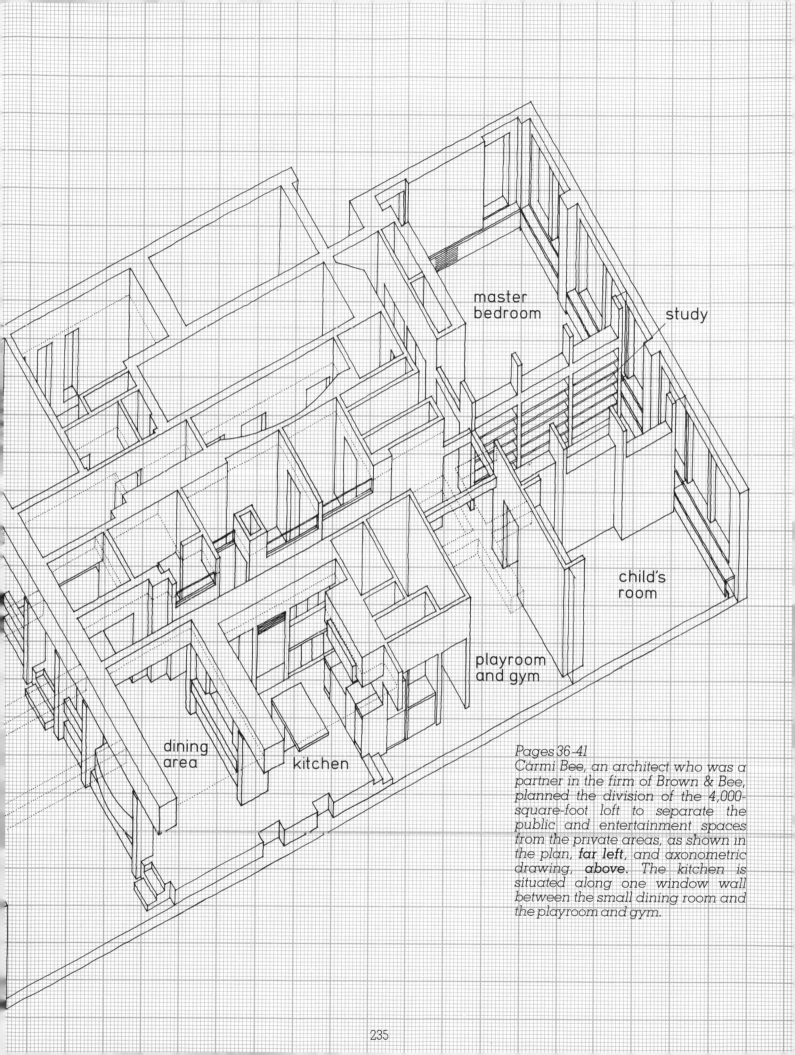

master
bedroom

study

child's
room

playroom
and gym

dining
area

kitchen

*Pages 36-41*
*Carmi Bee, an architect who was a*
*partner in the firm of Brown & Bee,*
*planned the division of the 4,000-*
*square-foot loft to separate the*
*public and entertainment spaces*
*from the private areas, as shown in*
*the plan, **far left**, and axonometric*
*drawing, **above**. The kitchen is*
*situated along one window wall*
*between the small dining room and*
*the playroom and gym.*

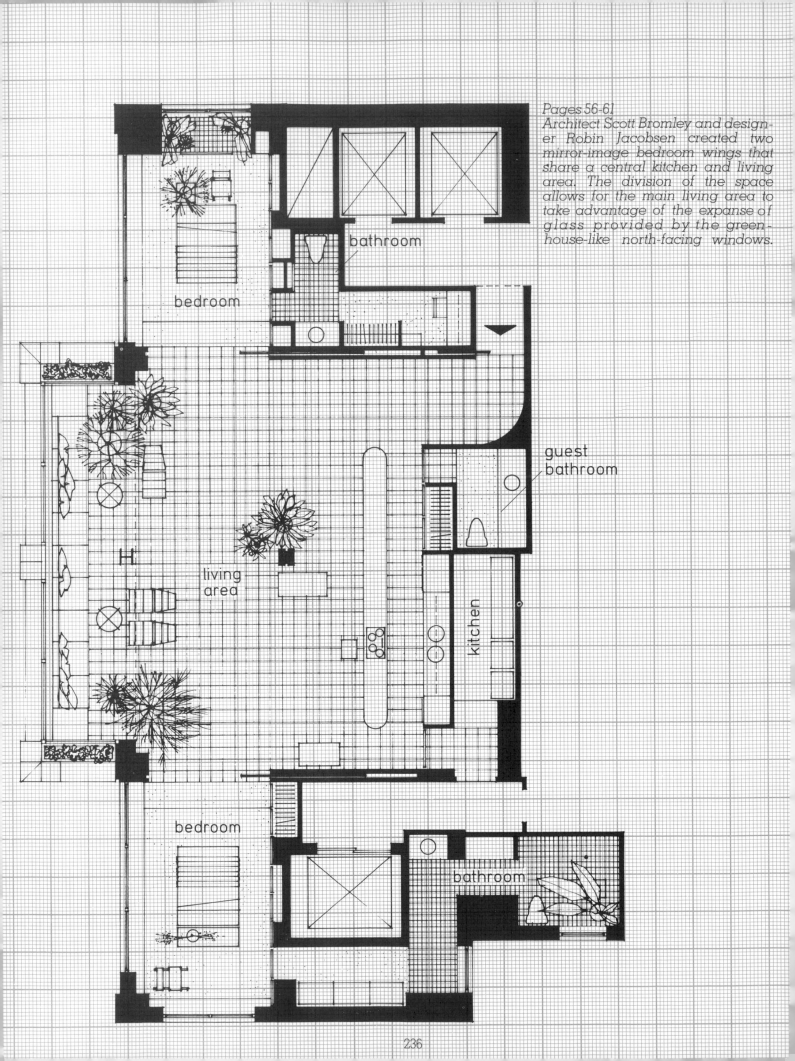

bathroom

Pages 56-61
*Architect Scott Bromley and design-
er Robin Jacobsen created two
mirror-image bedroom wings that
share a central kitchen and living
area. The division of the space
allows for the main living area to
take advantage of the expanse of
glass provided by the greenhouse-like north-facing windows.*

bedroom

guest
bathroom

living
area

kitchen

bedroom

bathroom

236

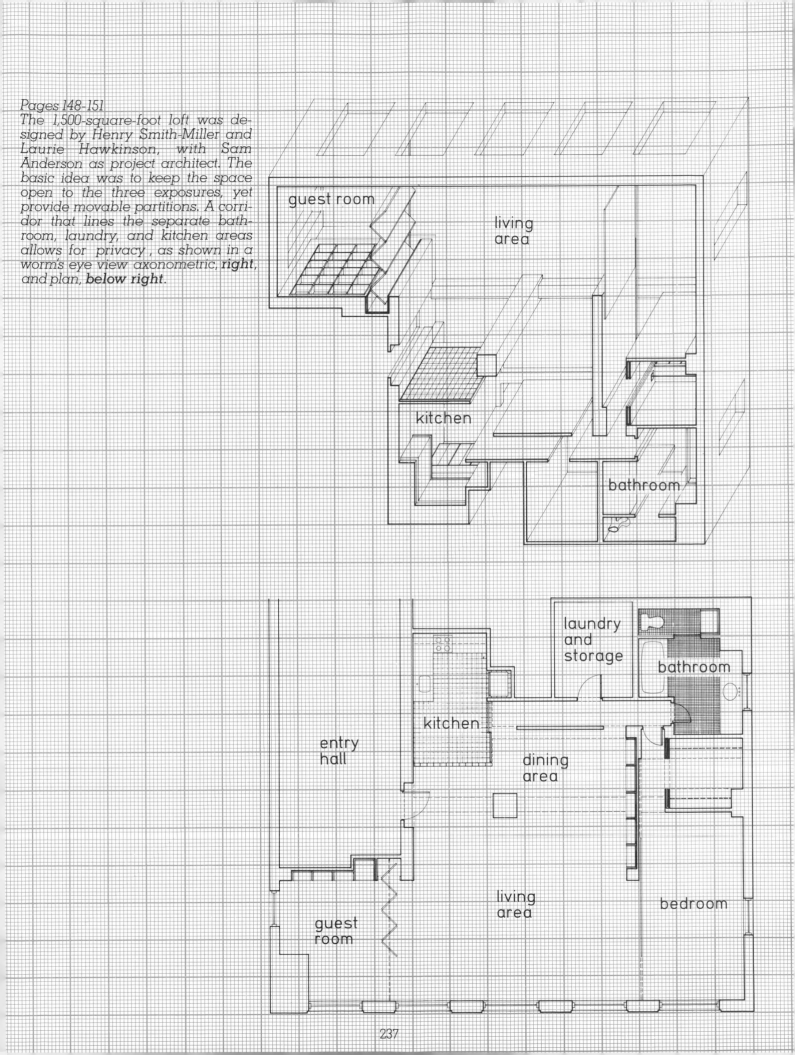

Pages 148-151
The 1,500-square-foot loft was designed by Henry Smith-Miller and Laurie Hawkinson, with Sam Anderson as project architect. The basic idea was to keep the space open to the three exposures, yet provide movable partitions. A corridor that lines the separate bathroom, laundry, and kitchen areas allows for privacy, as shown in a worm's eye view axonometric, *right*, and plan, **below right**.

guest room

living area

kitchen

bathroom

laundry and storage

bathroom

entry hall

kitchen

dining area

guest room

living area

bedroom

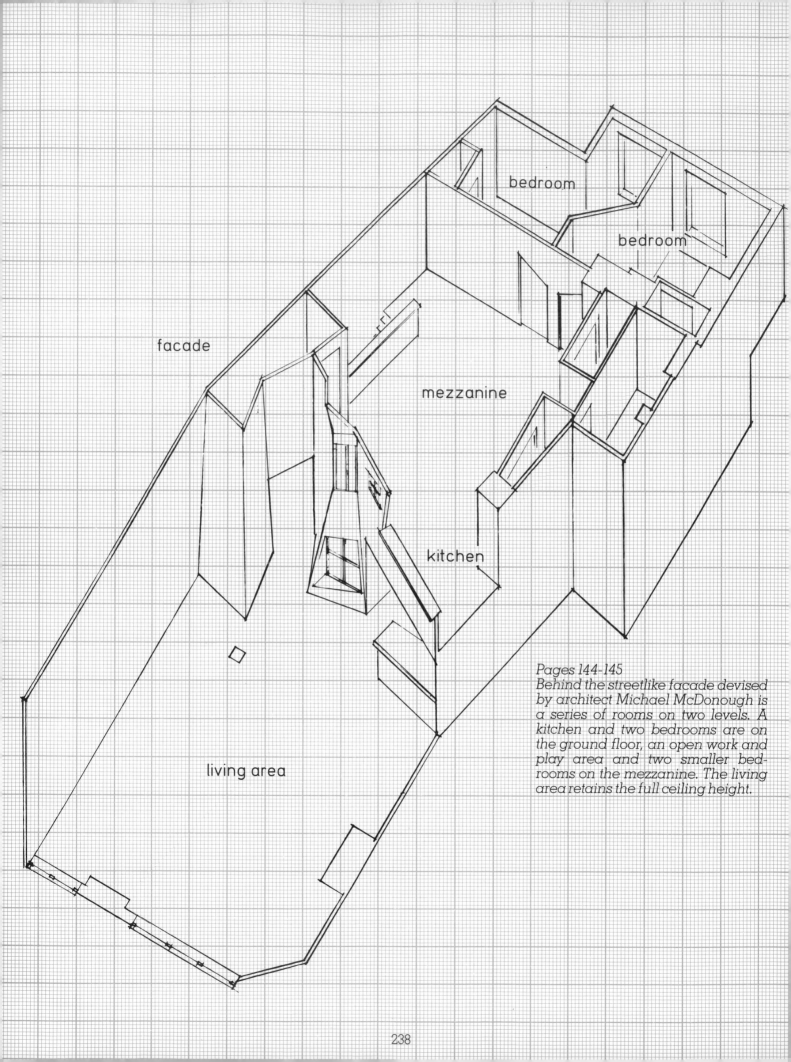

facade

bedroom

bedroom

mezzanine

kitchen

living area

Pages 144-145
*Behind the streetlike facade devised
by architect Michael McDonough is
a series of rooms on two levels. A
kitchen and two bedrooms are on
the ground floor, an open work and
play area and two smaller bedrooms on the mezzanine. The living
area retains the full ceiling height.*

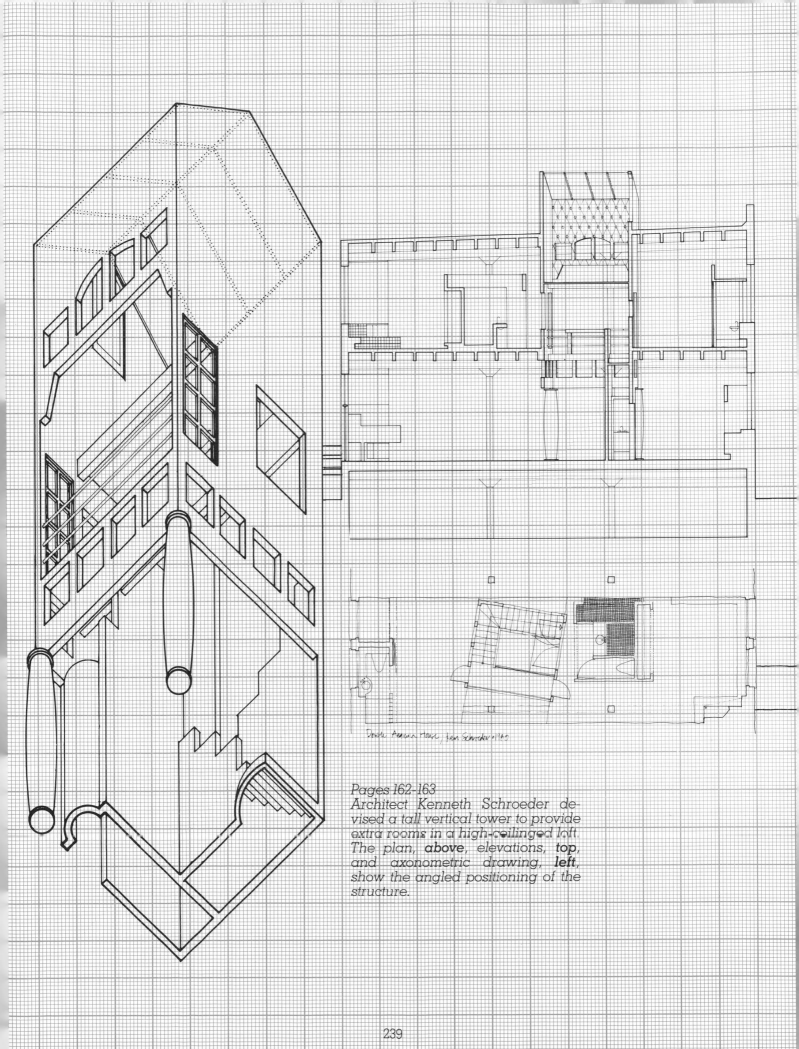

Double Armour House, Ken Schroeder © 1980

*Pages 162-163*
*Architect Kenneth Schroeder de-*
*vised a tall vertical tower to pro-*
*vide extra rooms in a high-ceilinged loft.*
*The plan, **above**, elevations, **top**,*
*and axonometric drawing, **left**,*
*show the angled positioning of the*
*structure.*

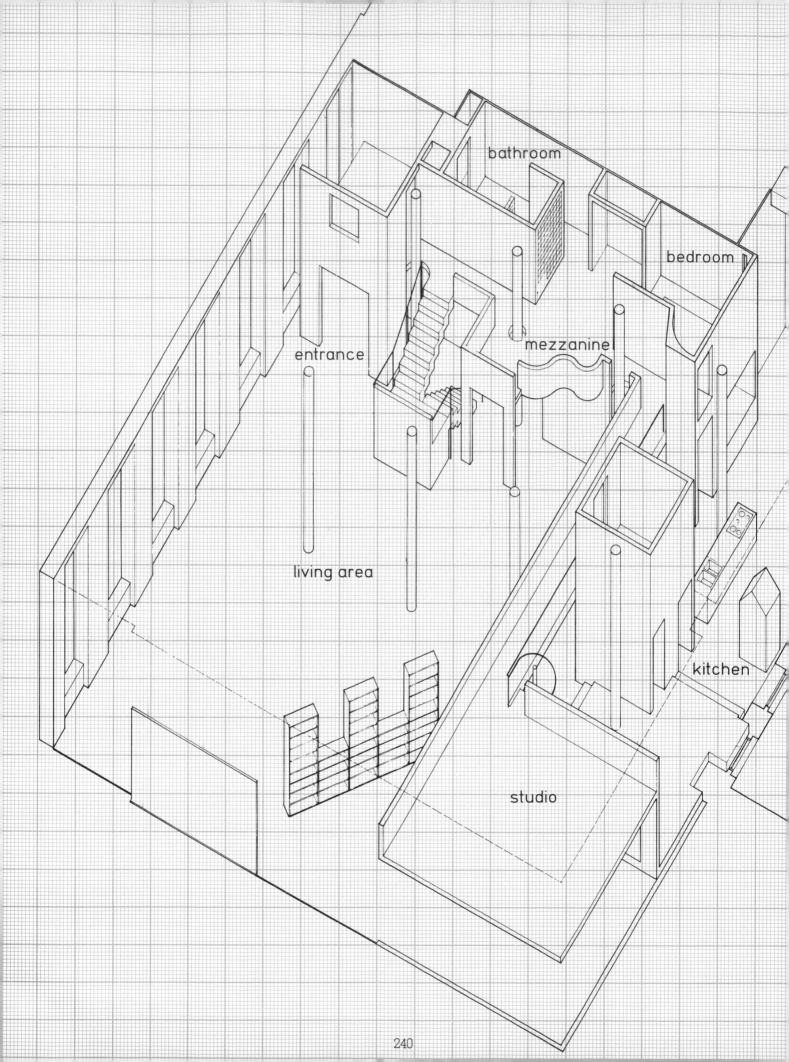

bathroom

bedroom

entrance

mezzanine

living area

kitchen

studio

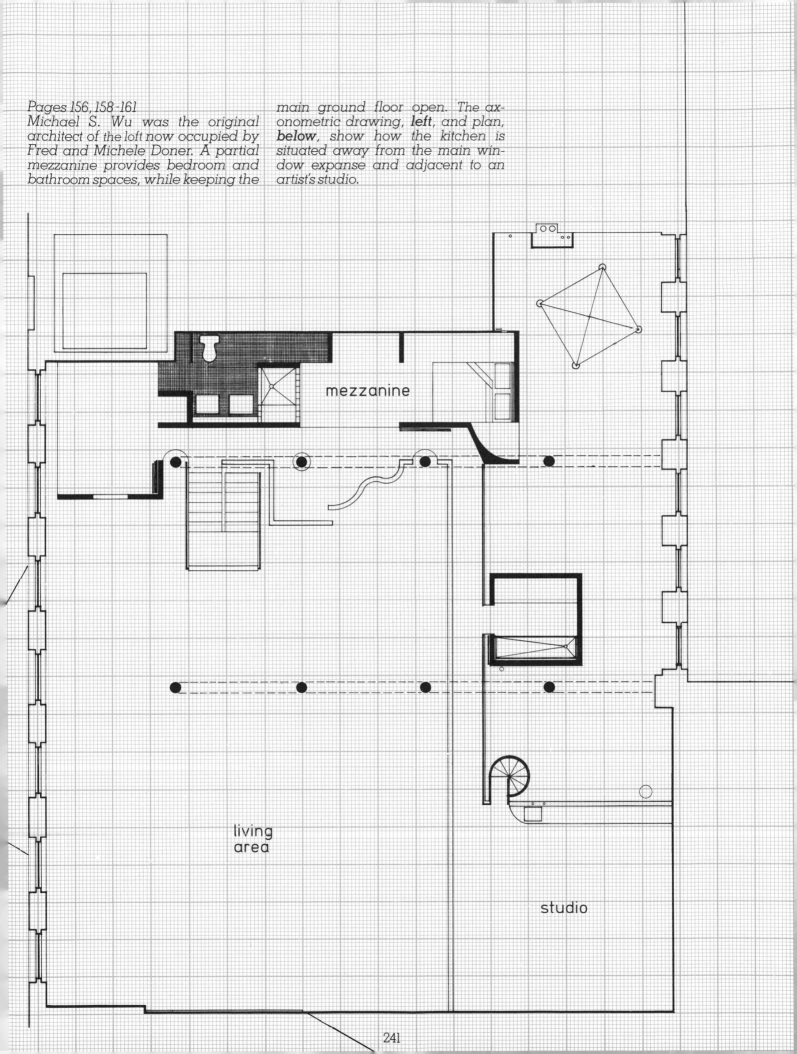

Pages 156, 158-161
Michael S. Wu was the original architect of the loft now occupied by Fred and Michele Doner. A partial mezzanine provides bedroom and bathroom spaces, while keeping the main ground floor open. The axonometric drawing, **left**, and plan, **below**, show how the kitchen is situated away from the main window expanse and adjacent to an artist's studio.

mezzanine

living
area

studio

241

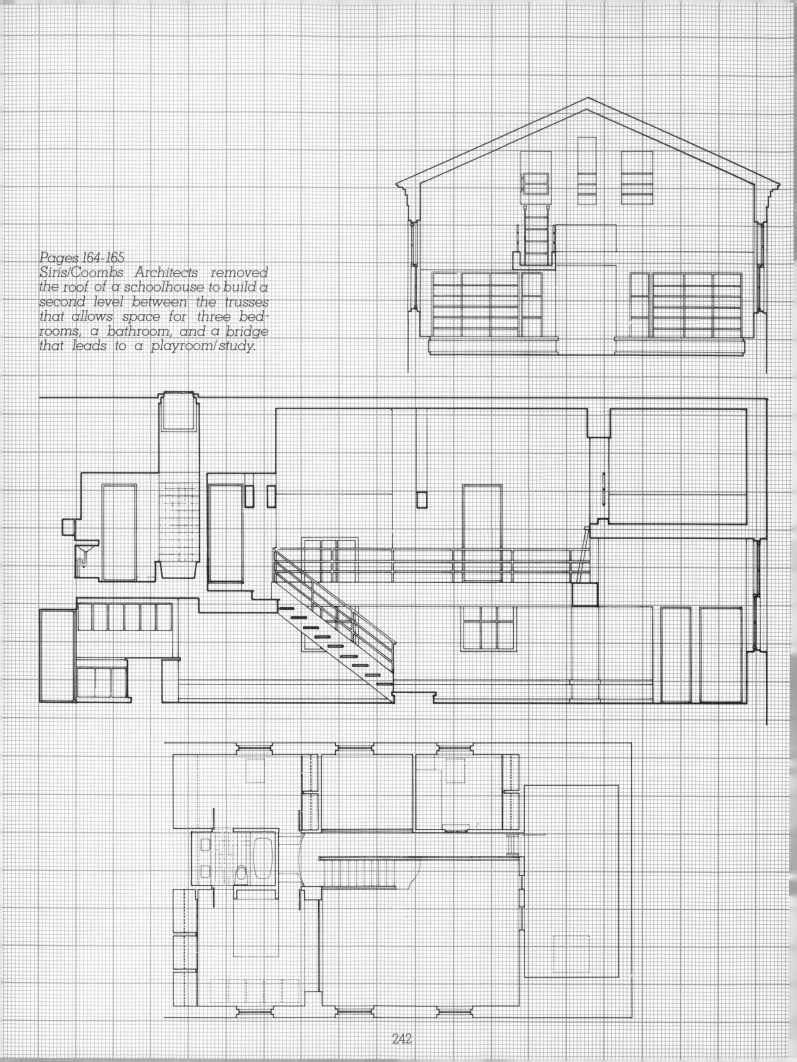

Pages 164-165
Siris/Coombs Architects removed the roof of a schoolhouse to build a second level between the trusses that allows space for three bedrooms, a bathroom, and a bridge that leads to a playroom/study.

Pages 172-173
A shallow mezzanine was interior
designer Juan Montoya's solution for
extra space in a long loft. Both levels
take advantage of the wide windows that face a river view.

living
area

kitchen

dining
area

bathroom

mezzanine
bedroom

UP

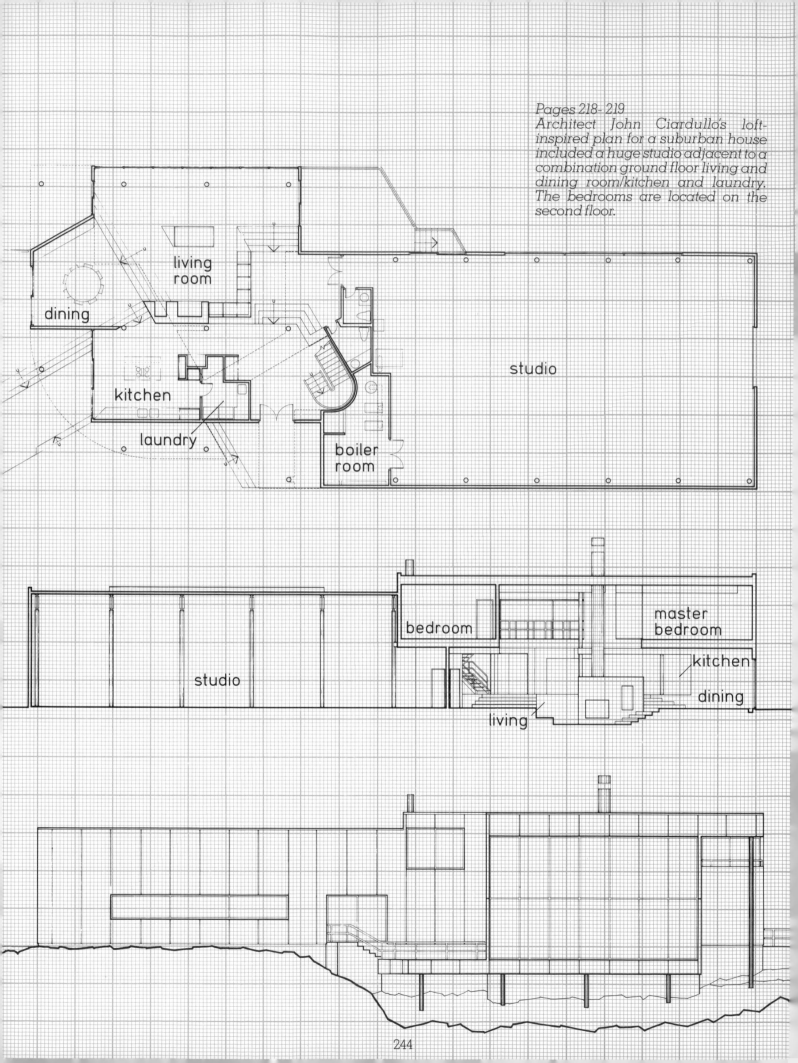

Pages 218- 219
Architect John Ciardullo's loft-
inspired plan for a suburban house
included a huge studio adjacent to a
combination ground floor living and
dining room/kitchen and laundry.
The bedrooms are located on the
second floor.

living
room

dining

studio

kitchen

laundry

boiler
room

bedroom

master
bedroom

studio

kitchen

living

dining

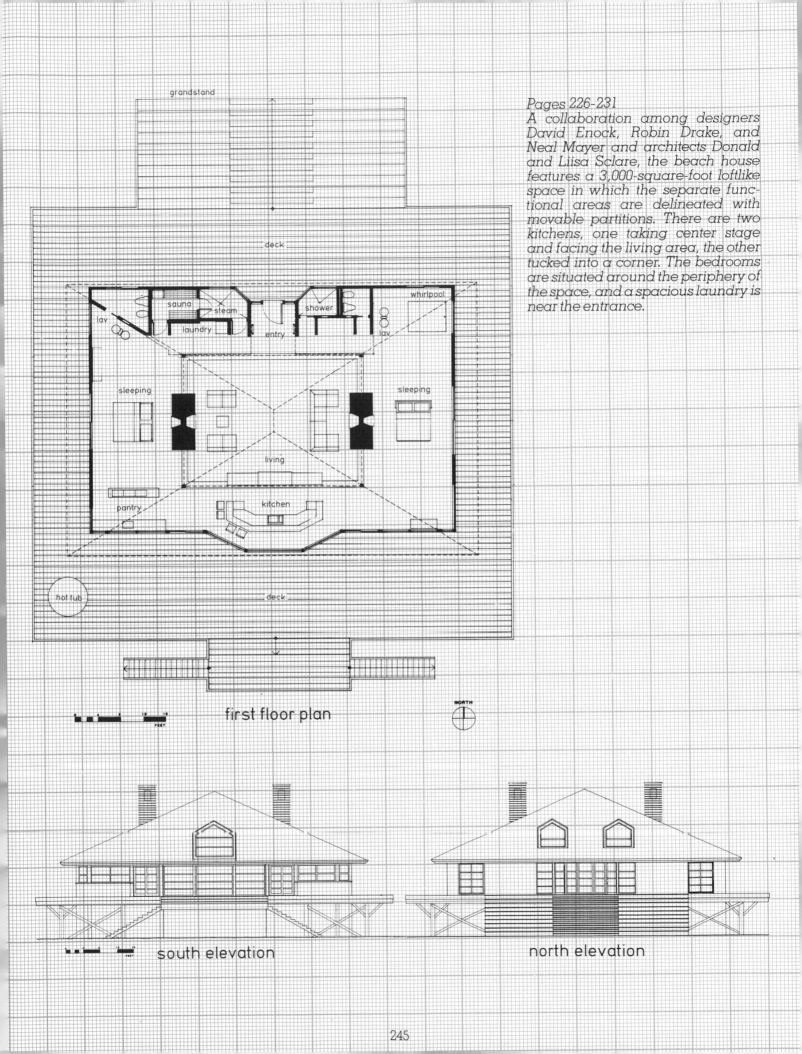

grandstand

deck

lav

sauna
steam
laundry

shower

whirlpool

entry

lav

sleeping

sleeping

living

pantry

kitchen

hot tub

deck

first floor plan

FEET

NORTH

Pages 226-231
A collaboration among designers
David Enock, Robin Drake, and
Neal Mayer and architects Donald
and Liisa Sclare, the beach house
features a 3,000-square-foot loftlike
space in which the separate functional areas are delineated with
movable partitions. There are two
kitchens, one taking center stage
and facing the living area, the other
tucked into a corner. The bedrooms
are situated around the periphery of
the space, and a spacious laundry is
near the entrance.

south elevation

north elevation

# PHOTOGRAPHY CREDITS

Page 2: The Bettman Archive; pages 4-5: The Bettman Archive; page 6: Roger Viollet; page 7, *top:* Butler's Wharf Ltd.; page 7, *bottom:* Museum of the City of New York; page 8: Courtesy of the New-York Historical Society; pages 8-9: The New York Public Library; pages 10-11: The Bettman Archive; page 12: Roger Viollet; page 13, *top:* The Bettman Archive; page 13, *bottom:* Louis Vuitton; pages 14-15: Courtesy of the New-York Historical Society; pages 16-17: Butler's Wharf Ltd.; page 18, *top:* Museum of the City of New York, *center,* Roger Viollet, *bottom,* Museum of the City of New York; Page 19: Roger Viollet; page 20: Roger Viollet; page 21, *top,* Roger Viollet; *bottom,* Time Magazine; page 22: Paul Hosefros/NYT Pictures; page 24, *top and center:* Gilles de Chabaneix, *bottom:* Liese Howard; page 25: Stafford Cliff; pages 26-27: Ken Kirkwood; page 28, *top left and right:* Antoine Bootz; page 28, *bottom:* Gilles de Chabaneix; page 29, Gilles de Chabaneix; pages 30-31: Langdon Clay; page 32: Oberto Gili; pages 34-35; Norman McGrath; pages 36-41: Gilles de Chabaneix; pages 42-45: Gilles de Chabaneix; pages 46-49: Rick Barnes; pages 50-55: Gilles de Chabaneix; pages 56-61: Gilles de Chabaneix; pages 62-67: Gilles de Chabaneix; pages 68-71: Robert Levin; page 72: Antoine Bootz; pages 74-77: Gilles de Chabaneix; pages 78-81: Gilles de Chabaneix; pages 82-85: Gilles de Chabaneix; pages 86-89: Antoine Bootz; pages 90-91: Gilles de Chabaneix; pages 92-95: Gilles de Chabaneix; page 96: S. Baker Vail; pages 98-99: Norman McGrath; pages 100-103: Gilles de Chabaneix; pages 104-105: Gilles de Chabaneix; pages 106-109: Gilles de Chabaneix; pages 110-111: Tim Street-Porter; pages 112-115: Frank Taeger; pages 116, 118-119: Marco de Valdivia; pages 120-123: Gilles de Chabaneix; pages 124-127: Antoine Bootz; page 128: Ralph Bogertman; pages 130-131: Tim Street-Porter; pages 132-133: Gilles de Chabaneix; pages 134-135: Gilles de Chabaneix; page 136: Steve Horvath; page 137: *top and center:* Nick Wheeler; *bottom:* Steve Horvath; pages 138-139: Donald Billinkoff; pages 140-143: Gilles de Chabaneix; pages 144-145: Gilles de Chabaneix; pages 146-147: Rick Barnes; pages 148-151: Marco de Valdivia; pages 152-153: Robert Levin; page 154: Gilles de Chabaneix; page 154: Antoine Bootz; pages 156, 158-161: Gilles de Chabaneix; pages 162-163: Peter Aaron (ESTO); pages 164-165: Karen Bussolini; pages 166-169: Tim Street-Porter; pages 170-171: Oberto Gili; pages 172-173: Robert Levin; page 174: Antoine Bootz; pages 176-179: Gilles de Chabaneix; pages 180-181: Gilles de Chabaneix; pages 182-185: Gilles de Chabaneix; pages 186-189: Tim Street-Porter, except page 187, *top left:* Ron Leighton; pages 190-193: Gilles de Chabaneix; pages 194-197: Gilles de Chabaneix; pages 198-199: Gilles de Chabaneix; pages 200-203: Gilles de Chabaneix; pages 204-205: Gilles de Chabaneix; page 206: Oberto Gili; page 208: Gilles de Chabaneix; page 209, *top left and right:* Gilles de Chabaneix, *center left:* Antoine Bootz, *center right,* Gilles de Chabaneix, *bottom left,* Jan Staller, *bottom right,* Tim Street-Porter; page 210: Gilles de Chabaneix; page 211: Studio Azzurro; page 212: Robert Levin; pages 214-217: Gilles de Chabaneix; pages 218-219: Robert Levin; pages 220-221: Gilles de Chabaneix; pages 222-225: Athos Lecce; pages 226-231: Antoine Bootz; page 232: Gilles de Chabaneix.

# INDEX

# INDEX